CW00517427

A JARVIS TAPESTRY

TUDOR TO VICTORIAN

PLOUGHING

BREAKING GROUND

HARROWING

SOWING

Gloria Jarvis Smith

A Jarvis Tapestry
First published in 2003

Published by Gloria Jarvis Smith,
The Bungalow, Tyler Close, Canterbury, Kent CT2 7BD

ISBN 0-9543656-0-7

Printed by Jenwood Printers Limited, Sheerness, Kent

ACKNOWLEDGEMENTS

The Centre for Buckinghamshire Studies for the transcription of the Last Will and Testament of Richard Jervis of Haddenham, 1557, and also for excerpts from "A Plan of the Manor of Soulbury" by Wm Woodward, 1769.

The Rev. C. Denham and Parish Council for the photograph of the fragment of fresco in St. Mary the Virgin, Haddenham.

The Buckinghamshire Genealogical Society for permission to reproduce my article, What was it like in the War, Grandfather? from Bucks Ancestor and also A Lady's Wardrobe 1735, and Oh, Grandpa, you led me a Dance!

The Society of Women Writers and Journalists for allowing me to reproduce from The Woman Journalist Margaret Crosland's Profile of me, with special thanks to her.

The black and white drawings on agriculture and warfare have as source The British Library.

The French Society of Archaeology for the list of William the Conqueror's companions in the Church of our Lady at Dives-Sur-Mer, Normandy.

Cover: Drawing of her grandfather, Val. H. Jarvis, by the author.

FOREWORD

Ah, memory...precious memory...for without grandfather casting his mind back to a Victorian childhood my family tree might not have got off the ground, and his own loveable grandfather would have remained in obscurity, leaving me the poorer......

CONTENTS

A descendant of this Buckinghamshire family tells their story

THE PAST IS OUR LOOKING GLASS

We are the sum total of our ancestors - I wish I could put a name to the author of this telling phrase, to give him his due. For with his concept in mind, how intriguing it is to contemplate the Last Will and Testament of some past relative in the knowledge that even the genes of the remotest forebears will be living on in those who came after - to influence looks, temperament, idiosyncracies and traits of character of the ones yet to come.

Nor must the maternal side be forgotten - that regiment of great grandmothers down the ages, fitting into the genealogical framework and introducing genes of their own lineage into the ever widening family circle - to prompt, how many times, the remark that someone in the throng ``is a Jarvis, all right!``

PLOUGHING

Are these distant souls aware of my efforts to trace them, I wonder? Hearing my cries for help, did they respond to the impasse my searches were in? For suddenly the way became clear, pointing to Haddenham, a village south-west of Aylesbury, in Buckinghamshire. Gradually there emerged a cavalcade of yeomen farming their freehold acres of arable and pasture, living their longish lives, seemingly physically fit. I got to know them through their Wills - so much so, that if I were to meet them one day - it would be just like greeting old friends. Indeed, the earliest Will, of 1557, is graphic enough to make its Richard Jervis and 16th century England spring to life off the parchment, conveying the picture of quite a comfortable home, with its head a widower who comes across as rather human. He was one of a long line of Richards - baptism of the eldest son with the name being observed till the turn of the 19th century, that is, on our branch of the Jarvis family of Haddenham.

1

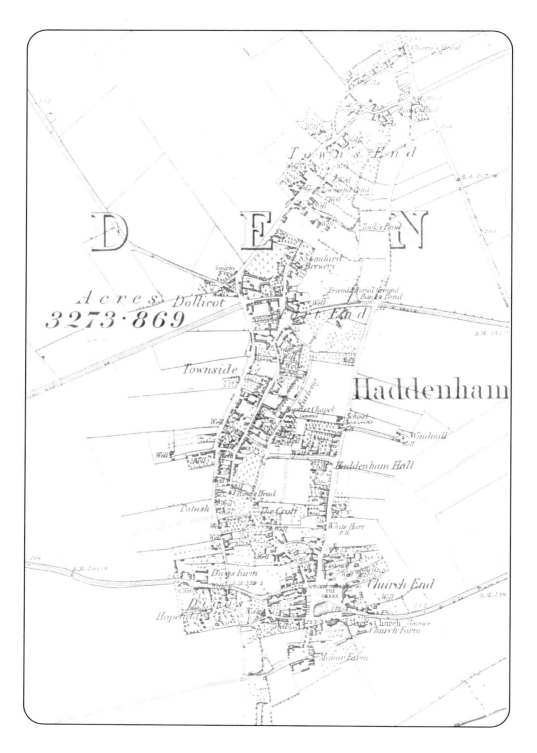

WHERE THERE'S A WILL

WHERE THERE'S A WILL.........there's a way of getting to the heart of its maker. Little clues in the expression of the wording can reveal a being as real and personable as on the day that shakey hand put signature - or mark - to parchment. Those occasional nuances in the script can point to a degree of love and esteem that the testator feels for his wife, or lack of regard for a son-in-law. Who can fail to warm to an 18th century Uncle John for naming his two geldings, ``Spark`` and ``Tinker``? Or, to Grandad Richard's bequest in 1692 of ``my best red bullock`` to his grandson, another Richard?

But it is through the land recorded in the document that one branch of the family can be traced from one generation to another. In fact, the land establishes the direct line. Furthermore, it can be double-checked in the Manorial Rolls, those accounts kept by the Lord or Lady of the Manor, to whom the beneficiary will have paid his dues on coming into his inheritance.

BREAKING GROUND   HARROWING   SOWING

It was through the land that I built up the Jarvis family tree - by comparing one Will with another. Nowdays, all parish records are held in the Record Office of a county town. Aylesbury's Record Office contains the Wills of each principal Haddenham Jarvis of the late 17th, the 18th, and early 19th centuries - not forgetting the Will already mentioned of the 16th century Richard. Drawn up in1557, the last year of Catholic Mary Tudor's reign, it was proved after his death the following year, when Protestant Bess came to the throne, enforcing a change of faith throughout the land. So what happened to Richard's rosary of red beads, I wonder? Destined for the old former vicar of Haddenham, did he preserve them in continuing to adhere to Rome in the secrecy of his closet? In this particular Will, an inventory of household goods vividly expresses ``hearth and home``. Furthermore, Richard's gilded goblet, silver spoons, and tester made from Arras hangings, suggest a grander past, perhaps a family originally of gentleman status - one rung higher than yeoman in the social scale.
These artefacts suggest the parcelling out of heirlooms to a large family circle. Each had his share.

There is a possible descent from John Gervays of Stoke Goldington, in the north-east tip of Bucks, in the 14th century. He inherited from his father-in-law, John de Morewell, an estate in Stoke Goldington, whose deeds were discovered among papers in the cellars of Gayhurst House - Gayhurst being the seat then of the de Nowers, one of whom married a Goldington heiress. John de Morewell was descended from the lordly Revell and Goldington families. It is quite likely that John Gervays is part of our heritage.

But this is only speculation for now--to be discussed further on in the book. I shall first deal with the authenticated version of the family tree that takes us with certainty to the mid-16th century.

It is obvious to point out--but by escaping as they must have done the scourge of the Black Death and other putrid plagues, our past kin have made survivors of us all--and through every extant Last Will and Testament they have left imprints on the passage of time--for which I am intensely grateful.

With insight into the Jarvis circumstances of the 17th and 18th centuries historian and genealogist, Eve McLaughlin, notes: "They must have been well-heeled for each family to set up more than one son as yeoman - as many as three in some cases - considering the land and livestock involved.", but by the 19th century life in the countryside had undergone a great change.

WORKMEN

A LONDON STREET
DURING THE BLACK DEATH

WORKMEN.

OUR NAME OF JARVIS

In the 11th century ordinary people had still not acquired surnames, but by the 15th century they had - somewhere in between it happened.

The name JARVIS is derived from the Norman personal name of Gervase. In fact, the spelling of JARVIS in early parish registers is often Gervis as late as well into the17th century, and even Garvis.

Being the name of a saint (martyred under the Emperor Diocletian), GERVASE was in circulation throughout Europe in the Middle Ages, under different spellings: HERVAS in Spanish; GERVASINI in Italian; VASON in Venetian; GERVASING in Low German - to name but a few of the variations. In England, GERVASE, the 12th century chronicler of Christ Church, Canterbury, springs to mind.

Nowadays, there is quite a sprinkling of GERVAIS in the French telephone directory.

Not long ago, I came across, in the public reference library in Aylesbury, the Dictionnaire des Noms de Famille et Prénoms de France, published by Larousse (1951). It lists GERVAIS as a surname (with the note that rarely is it used as a Christian name). Interestingly, it gives variations of the spelling in the South of France: GERVEX (Limousin); GERVAZY (Puy de Dome); GERVASI, -ASY -AZY (Provencale forms); but even more fascinating is the version in Puy de Dome patois: DZARVAJE ... now does it not have the ring of JARVIS when pronounced?

WEEDING.   REAPING.   THRESHING

Incidentally, as a pet name in French it becomes GERVOT!

5

JARVIS of HADDENHAM

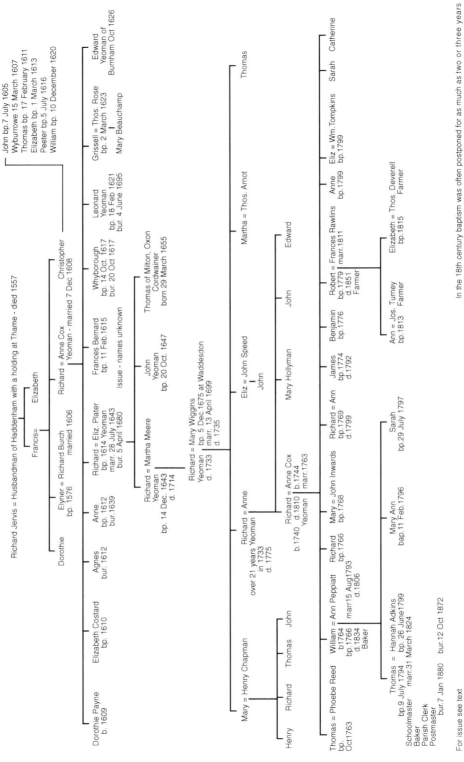

Richard Jervis = Husbandman of Haddenham with a holding at Thame - died 1557

John bp.7 July 1605
Wyburrowe 15 March 1607
Thomas bp. 17 February 1611
Elizabeth bp. 1 March 1613
Peeter bp.5 July 1616
William bp. 10 December 1620

Edward
Yeoman of
Burnham Oct 1626

Grissell = Thos. Rose
bp. 2 March 1623
Mary Beauchamp

Leonard
Yeoman
bp. 18 Feb 1621
bur. 4 June 1695

Richard = Anne Cox
Yeoman - married 7 Dec 1608

Whyborough
bp. 14 Oct. 1617
bur. 20 Oct 1617

Frances Bernard
bp. 11 Feb. 1615

Issue - names unknown

Thomas of Milton, Oxon
Cordwainer
born 29 March 1655

John
Yeoman
bp. 20 Oct. 1647

Francis =   Elizabeth

Elyner = Richard Burch
bp. 1576   married 1606

Anne
bp. 1612
bur.1639

Richard = Eliz. Plater
bp. 1614 Yeoman
marr. 28 July 1643
bur. 5 April 1680

Richard = Martha Meere
Yeoman
bp. 14 Dec. 1643
d. 1714

Richard = Mary Wiggins
Yeoman   bp. 5 Dec.1675 at Waddesdon
d. 1733   marr. 13 April 1699
d. 1735

Dorothie

Dorothie Payne
b. 1609

Elizabeth Costard
bp. 1610

Agnes
bur. 1612

Thomas

Martha = Thos. Arnot

Eliz = John Speed
John

Mary = Henry Chapman

Richard = Anne
over 21 years Yeoman
in 1733
d. 1775

Edward

John

Mary Hollyman

Richard = Anne Cox
b.1740 d.1810 b.1744
Yeoman   marr.1763

Catherine

Sarah

Eliz = Wm.Tompkins
bp.1799

Anne
bp.1799

Robert = Frances Rawlins
bp.1779   marr.1811
d.1851
Farmer

Benjamin
bp.1776

James
bp.1774
d.1792

Richard = Ann
bp.1769
d.1799

Mary = John Inwards
bp.1768

Elizabeth = Thos. Deverell
bp.1815   Farmer

Ann = Jos. Turney
bp.1813   Farmer

Sarah
bp.29 July 1797

Mary Ann
bap.11 Feb.1796

Henry   Richard   Thomas   John

William = Ann Peppiatt
b1764
bp.1766 marr15 Aug1793
d.1834 d.1806
Baker

Richard
bp.1766

Thomas = Phoebe Reed
bp.
Oct1763

Thomas = Hannah Adkins
bp.9 July 1794 marr.31 March 1824
d.1872
Schoolmaster bur.7 Jan 1880 bur.12 Oct 1872
Baker
Parish Clerk
Postmaster

For issue see text

In the 18th century baptism was often postponed for as much as two or three years
so that several of the same brood would be baptised together.

6

"...WHOSE LIMBS WERE MADE IN ENGLAND"

"In the name of God Amen the 16th day of May in the year of our Lord 1557 I Richard Jervis of Haddenham in the county of Buckinghamshire husbandman of whole mind and good rememberance make this my last Will and Testament".

The survival of that document has provided the earliest known record of our direct forebears. But despite the fourteen generation divide, that distant grandfather is as real to me as if he were alive today. Because of this feeling of familiarity he is my elected point of departure, however much it may appear a "back-to-frontism" to come forward in time and not the reverse. It may serve to stress that some part of his personality is perpetuated through the genes of his descendants, down to us and those to come.

"...first I bequeath my soul to God Almighty to our Lady Saint Mary and all the holy company of heaven..."

What a splendid ring has "all the holy company of heaven", conjuring up the fresco, perhaps an apotheosis, high in the nave of St. Mary's Church in Haddenham, and of which only a fragment remains - an archangel blowing a trumpet, painted in green, yellow, vermilion and black. A scene to stir the imagination of Richard and his fellow worshippers.

Richard's Last Will and Testament, written in the Catholic England of Mary Tudor, recalls the pre-Reformation way of death. It is by way of so-called "indulgences" - that

by leaving money to the church, Richard is promised remission of his sins, which must have given him spiritual comfort in the face of approaching death, to the benefit, also, to altar, bells and fabric, apparently in need of repair.

One sin in particular bothers him - "forgotten tithes", as he nicely puts it to justify more than an occasional lapse in handing over to the church one tenth of the farm produce expected of him annually. But by leaving 12d for the upkeep of the high altar, a penitent Richard hopes to redress the balance. Yet, a peccadillo here and there only reveals the human side of the man. Besides, claiming a poor memory is endearingly funny, since at the outset of the Will he professes to be of "good remembrance" - a touch of naivety that makes him more lovable.

Infirm he might have been, and even close to death, for the Will was proved the following year on the 21st of November 1558.

The Will is in a perfect state of conservation, bound into a volume of similar documents at the Bucks Record Office in Aylesbury. The ink looks as fresh as if the scribe had just finished his task. However much that stylised court hand of the Tudor legal profession leaves one alphabetically challenged, yet viewed through half-closed eyes it can be seen for its abstract qualities alone - and then that bold decorative statement rises to the level of a work of art.

Richard Jervis was of the yeoman class which in those days meant a countryman, farmer,of middling social status. The yeoman's legendary attributes would have most probably escaped his ken - not for years yet was Shakespeare to write those immortal lines with which Henry V rouses his troops before Harfleur:

"And you, good yeomen,
Whose limbs were made in England, show us here
The mettle of your pasture; let us swear
That you are worth your breeding, which I doubt not;
For there is none of you so mean and base,
That hath not noble lustre in your eyes".

Stirring words - especially to me - aware that the seed of Richard Jervis flowed on in generations of Bucks yeomen down to the 19th century. But his forefathers, too, must have been of that ilk - with perhaps, who knows - descent from Gervase, the 13th century parson farmer of Sherington (north-east of the county) which, if proven, thereby would form a link with Normandy and knightly circles around the Conquest.

Pictorially, Richard's Will throws light on his 16th century household. One takes him for a widower. The next of kin are Francis and Elizabeth, son and daughter. It is clear that the boy has almost reached manhood, seeing that his father names him as executor "if the law will give him leave by age". Otherwise, Robert Williamson, clerk and former vicar of Haddenham, is appointed to supervise, which he is eventually called on to do, and for his pains inherits - besides a rosary and a spit - a feather bed and bolster, a pillow and a pair of sheets which should have seen him comfortably bedded for the rest of his life.

"The covering that Master Grene hath" vaguely suggests a loan to an impoverished soul in the community, like a monk cast adrift after the dissolution of the monasteries. That plethora of feather beds, diaper linen, coverlets, pillows,bolsters and towels - to be divided between Francis and Elizabeth - reminds me how important a feature the bed was - in life, for procreation - arriving full circle in death. In fact death will have come to Richard as he had always slept, in a half-sitting position, propped up by pillows. The bed itself was probably shorter than today's. People then were not in the habit of stretching out full length, as it was thought that a rush of blood to the head would prove fatal.

If the master-bedroom was the one at the rear, referred to as "the backer" - there stood the bed canopied with a tester ("it is of arras work and was made for hangings"); then under this vestige of an early 15th century tapestry slept Richard, mirrored in the prosperity of a past generation, when the walls of the best rooms were adorned with the "Cloth of Arras" representing hunting scenes in allegorical style. This may have been the bed in which Richard, bedridden at the last, dictated his Will.

There arises the question of the man's age. At a guess, I put him around 57 to 60, born and swaddled in the latter part of the reign of HenryVII. The average for marriage among the yeoman class was 25 to 28 years. If, at the drafting of the Will, Francis the son were 17, it would make the lad's birth in 1530. But supposing he had an elder brother, since deceased? For the possibility arises since the tradition of naming the first son Richard persists in this our line until the mid-18th century, and had appeared in local records of the 15th century. In fact, father Richard Jervis might have started a family in the 1520s - or even wed late in life, attaining the good old age for those days of 65 to 70 (the Wills of subsequent generations show many long-livers in all branches of the Jarvis family, down to the present day).

It is obvious that "Margaret my kinswoman who is with me" is a cousin or niece invited to play a motherly role in the houshold. Richard's kindly feeling towards her and sense of fairness comes through the wording which stresses that Margaret must be looked after. For keeping house and tending the children she earned his gratitude. His brother's offspring will get gifts of money, while his poorest relations can expect any surplus clothing once Francis and Elizabeth have had their pick. Godchildren are remembered, too, and even the poor of Haddenham are to have 20s distributed among them, with the pious hope that they daily pray for his soul - and they probably went down on their knees for their benefactor.

In a flash of inward eye, one can see the little family at table. It would have been laid with one of several diaper cloths, napkins and the luxury of a choice of 13 silver spoons, mazers and bowls, and a Tudor repast that had been prepared by Margaret and borne in by her or a servant. It will be Richard who will put his lips to the partly gilded goblet - another heirloom that complements the silver spoons.

In speculating on the food that Margaret was likely to have prepared we know English cooks were commended for roasted meats but that few vegetables accompanied the dish. In fact, doctors today tell us that a surfeit of protein hastened the death of Henry VIII whose diet was deprived of vitamins through lack of vegetables (although cabbage was added to the pottage). According to that 16th century traveller, Fynes Moryson: "... venison pasty is a dainty.. and howsoever hares are thought to nourish melancholy, yet they are eaten as venison both roast and boiled. They have also great plenty of conies (rabbits) the flesh thereof is fat, tender and more delicate than any I have eaten in other parts". Brawn was a meat dish peculiar to England. And as for bread, it was often a mixture of different kinds of grain - "The Englishman eats barley and rye brown bread, and prefers it to white as abiding longer in the stomach", just as today we find it more satisfying. Barley was also used in the making of beer, which was regularly drunk at breakfast. Folk had big appetites. Said one: "I know not how we should eat any more, unless we should borrow other bellyes!".

The chief meal of the day was dinner eaten at noon or an hour earlier, supper around five hours later. For it was "early to bed" and spare the candles, so as "early to rise" with a good day's work ahead, especially in the longer daylight hours of summer.

I should like to ask Richard if he put on his "harness girdle" as a matter of course (there is one bequeathed to each of the children). "Harness" meant armour - "girdle" meant hip belt from which weapons hung on hangers - needed in hunting, perhaps, and to offset danger from vagrants.

Elizabeth may have hung keys on hers, chatelaine style. Much of her day would have been taken up spinning and helping Margaret to mend any worn workaday clothes like doublet and hose and sundry linen. There was dusting and sweeping to be done and cushions to beat. In springtime it was the moment to take out the kirtles and mantles from the chests to spread them in the sun in the garden to air and beat with little sticks.Spots and stains had to be removed with some special cocoction, and there was always the odd moth or flea to pounce on. Richard's Will implies that his wardrobe was fairly extensive: "...that my apparel be bestowed the chief to my children and the rest to such of my kin as to be the poorest". A kirtle bequeathed to Margaret would have reached the ankles to lend dignity befitting an older man.

Husbanding those acres of wheat, barley and peas, rearing the nucleus of farm animals such as the five cows, two oxen, four weaned calves, thirteen sheep, three mares and three horses should have been encompassed with ease and the use of farm gear mentioned, with, one supposes, a shepherd and labourer or two.

As to his spiritual needs, Richard's faith was bolstered by familiar symbols in his devotions such as his Agnus Dei - blessed by the Pope, perhaps - and the red stone beads that he told on his knees in the Lady Chapel of Haddenham church or intimacy of home; such an emblem was dubbed in 1533 as " The Mystick sweet Rosary of the Faiythful Soul". All such comforts would be swept away by the end of the following year, for Protestant Bess did not suffer Catholicism lightly.

Richard's life followed the same seasonal pattern as his ancestors. But who were they? And how many generations of Richard Jervis families had been already baptised in the font of Haddenham church? Parish registers were not kept before 1538, and if any existed as early in Haddenham, none had survived the disastrous fire that eventually destroyed a large number of records in more recent times.

The wording of Richard's Will gives an insight into his thoughts and character. This dear grandfather comes over the centuries as a just man, whose paternalism merits the worthy burial he expected of his son - "to honourably bury me".

The act of putting his seal to the Will gives us our last contact with that living being. Yet, since this document survives - then, happily, does much of Richard - Tudor farmer of the Marian age and almost an Elizabethian.

THE WILL OF RICHARD JERVIS 1557
Punctuated and with modern spellings

For words marked * see glossary.

In the name of God Amen the 16th day of may in the year of our Lord God 1557 I Richard Jervis of Haddenham in the county of Bucks husbandman of whole mind and good rememberance make this my last will and testament.

In manner and form following first I bequeath my soul to God Almighty to our Lady Saint Mary and to all the holy company of heaven and my body to be buried in the church yard of Haddenham aforesaid and my mortuary as the Law doth require Item I bequeath to the Cathedral church of Lincoln 4d Item to the repair of the church at Haddenham and the bells 12d Item to the high altar in the same church for Tithes forgotten 12d Item to the church of Thame 12d to the high altar in the same church for Tithes forgotten 12d Item I will that Fraunces my son have the house I dwell in in Haddenham with the appurtenances And if he die before he come to age I will then that it come to Elisabeth my daughter Item if my son do sell it I will then that my daughter Elisabeth if she be able to purchase it have it before another so it be for her self and her heirs Item I will that the said Fraunces have my hold (?holding) at Thame Item to the said Fraunces a goblet parcel (partly) gilt, 10 silver spoons & my best mazer* & harness girdle* Item to the said Fraunces 2 ?cope* of oxen, 3 kyne (cows), 3 horses, 2 mares, 2 weanling ?calfes, 9 sheep Item to the said Fraunces my Cart & cart (ha...) plough and plough gear and such stuff as do belong unto husbandry Item to Elisabeth my daughter the house that John Hunt doth dwell in and she to pay unto my son & his heirs one penny by the year and my son & his heirs to pay the rent unto the lord for the same house / and so be that my son chance to sell the hold (?holding) where I now dwell I will then that there be laid unto the same house where John Hunt doth dwell willed to my said daughter one acre in every field Item I will unto the said Elisabeth 2 kyne (cows), 2 weanling calves, 4 sheep, my young mare colt Item to the said Elisabeth 3 silver spoons, my little mazers and one harness girdle* & a pair of beles (?bellows) Item to the said Elisabeth an acre of wheat one acre of barley one acre of peas and if chance that I die at such time as any of the said grains be not sown for her use such as then/there be not sown Item Agnus Dei Item to Margaret my Kinswoman which is with me a brass pot & pan of the middlesort, 2 candlesticks, 2 platters, 2 dishes, 2 saucers, one pair of sheets, 2 bushels of wheat, 3 of malt, one bushel of peas & 10s in money & a kirtle* Item to every child of my brother... in money 12d Item to every one of my godchildren 4d Item to the poor people of Haddenham 20s Item to Fraunces my son 4 featherbeds with bolsters, one pair of blankets, 6 pairs of sheets, 6 diaper* napkins & a diaper tablecloth, one diaper towel, a towel plain cloth, 3 table cloths, the covering lined that I had of doctor godrike, the covering which is best save twayne (?3rd best), 3 pillows & the tester* in the backer (?rear) chamber it is of arras work & and was first made for hangings Item to Elisabeth my daughter 2 featherbeds the one whereof 1 will be of the better sort, 2 bolsters, one pair of blankets, 2 pair sheets, 6 diaper napkins, 2 diaper tables, a towell of plain, 2 table cloths, the covering which Mr Grene hath & one of the coverings in the backer (rear) chamber, 2 pillows & a tester and a christening sheet

Item to Robert Willamson clerk late vicar of Haddenham a featherbed and a bolster, a pillow, a pair of beads of stone of Red colour (?a rosary), one pair of sheets and one spit Item I will that such brass pewter & kitchen stuff as is not bequeathed be thus divided (my son Fraunces to have 2 parts thereof and my daughter Elisabeth the third) Item I will that if either of my said children die before they come to age then the part of him or her so dying go to the other and if they both die that half thereof be sold & the money thereof arising be given to the poor to pray for my soul and my friends and the rest to be divided to my brothers children willing that my kinswoman Margaret be specially remembered amongst them Item I will that my apparell be bestowed the chief to my children and the rest to such of my kin as to be poorest The rest of all my goods not bequeathed I give & bequeath to Fraunces my son to pay my debts & honestly (honourably) to bury me whom I do make my sole executor if the Law will give him leave by age/and if it will not I ordain my executor to join with him Robert Willamson clerk afore named to see this my last will and testament fulfilled & proved willing him to have setting and letting of such ?gro... as shall come to my children till they come to the age & the profits therof to be employed to the most profit of my said children and such stuff as shall appertain unto them not to commit to any or take to him without sufficient bond for the surety thereof And if the law permit my said son to have the execution of this my will and testament then I do ordain the said Robert Willamson the supervisor of this my said will & testament In witness thereof I have subscribed this with my own hand and put my seal the day and year above written.

Proved xxI november in the year 1558 before Master May and committed to administration of the executor as above Sworn personally by the said Robert Willamson (his) attorney Dated etc.

SHEEP FARM.

14

Glossary

* mazer

A bowl, drinking cup or goblet, without a foot, originally made of hardwood but later of various metals.

* harness girdle

Harness = armour.
Girdle = hip belt from which weapons were suspended on hangers - often ornamental.

* cope of oxen

A cop is the beam placed between a pair of draught oxen, so perhaps a cope of oxen is a pair of oxen.

* lachehoukes

Meaning is not known - may refer to door latch hooks or possibly to hooks for hanging meat (a latch pan is a dripping pan). Latch can also mean a noose or snare; lache can mean a barn. Latch is also sometimes used for leach, meaning to cause a liquid to percolate through some material.

* agnus dei

Figure of a lamb bearing a cross and flag; a cake or wax stamped with such a figure and blessed by the Pope.

* kirtle

Garment worn by both sexes but mainly by women. Probably a woman's gown or outer petticoat or a jacket.

* diaper

Twilled linen cloth woven with diamond patterns. Used for napkins, towels and tablecloths.

* tester

Ceiling of a bed, made of wood or fabric.

Courtesy of the Centre for Buckinghamhire Studies

Descendants of Catherine Helen Jarvis, daughter of James Jarvis

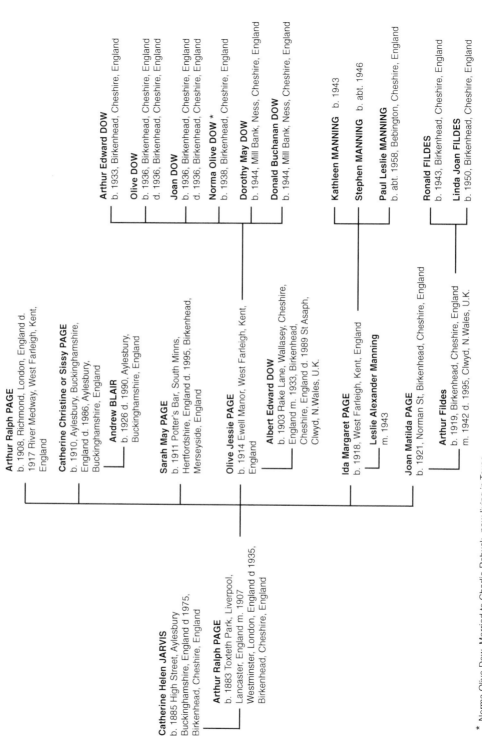

Catherine Helen JARVIS
b. 1885 High Street, Aylesbury, Buckinghamshire, England d 1975, Birkenhead, Cheshire, England

Arthur Ralph PAGE
b. 1883 Toxteth Park, Liverpool, Lancaster, England m. 1907 Westminster, London, England d 1935, Birkenhead, Cheshire, England

Arthur Ralph PAGE
b. 1908, Richmond, London, England d. 1917 River Medway, West Farleigh, Kent, England

Catherine Christine or Sissy PAGE
b. 1910, Aylesbury, Buckinghamshire, England d. 1986, Aylesbury, Buckinghamshire, England

Andrew BLAIR
b. 1926 d. 1990, Aylesbury, Buckinghamshire, England

Sarah May PAGE
b. 1911 Potter's Bar, South Minns, Hertfordshire, England d 1995, Birkenhead, Merseyside, England

Olive Jessie PAGE
b. 1914 Ewell Manor, West Farleigh, Kent, England

Albert Edward DOW
b. 1903 Rake Lane, Wallasey, Cheshire, England m. 1933, Birkenhead, Cheshire, England d. 1989 St Asaph, Clwyd, N.Wales, U.K.

Arthur Edward DOW
b. 1933, Birkenhead, Cheshire, England

Olive DOW
b. 1936, Birkenhead, Cheshire, England
d. 1936, Birkenhead, Cheshire, England

Joan DOW
b. 1936, Birkenhead, Cheshire, England
d. 1936, Birkenhead, Cheshire, England

Norma Olive DOW *
b. 1938, Birkenhead, Cheshire, England

Dorothy May DOW
b. 1944, Mill Bank, Ness, Cheshire, England

Donald Buchanan DOW
b. 1944, Mill Bank, Ness, Cheshire, England

Ida Margaret PAGE
b. 1918, West Farleigh, Kent, England

Leslie Alexander Manning
m. 1943

Kathleen MANNING   b. 1943

Stephen MANNING   b. abt. 1946

Paul Leslie MANNING
b. abt. 1958, Bebington, Cheshire, England

Joan Matilda PAGE
b. 1921, Norman St, Birkenhead, Cheshire, England

Arthur Fildes
b. 1919, Birkenhead, Cheshire, England
m. 1942 d. 1995, Clwyd, N.Wales, U.K.

Ronald FILDES
b. 1943, Birkenhead, Cheshire, England

Linda Joan FILDES
b. 1950, Birkenhead, Cheshire, England

* Norma Olive Dow, Married to Charlie Robuck, now living in Texas

16

A WINTER'S TALE

WHAT SPARKED IT OFF

It was a bright December day when I brought Nora and Charlie to Haddenham. She is a long lost second cousin from Texas whom I had discovered in researching our family origins - for she, too, descended from the same line of Buckinghamshire yeoman. Through the centuries our farming forebears had looked across the same village green with its duckpond - and seized any opportunity to forget to pay their tithes at the barn looming huge beyond. The church had witnessed all their joys and sorrows in the baptisms, marriages and burials descending the family tree.

Just then, my mind travelled back in time to single out perhaps such a day in 1608 - the wedding of our 9x great-grandparents, Richard and Ann. Once home, it did not take me long to fathom why they had chosen to marry as late as winter, the firstborn was already on the way, due the following March. It was not unusual to consummate the union beforehand, it seems, without precluding any shyness on the bride's part at the nuptials.

Gradually my imagination conjured up the betrothal and the wedding feast from the scant information to hand in the parish register, such as relevant dates. and the names of siblings, nephews and nieces - not to mention Richard's grandfather's Will which lists the family heirlooms handed down. Knowledge of the traditional denouement of the marriage and jollities does the rest - stored in the memory if one has been a devotee of history all through life. And by now the bride and groom had taken my fancy......

WEAVING

BEGGAR

SHOP.

Norma Dow Robuck, long lost cousin descended from Catherine Jarvis, with husband Charlie, living in Texas.

THE JACOBEAN WEDDING

It is the year 1608 and young Rycharde's fancy lightly turns to love... time the eldest son of Francis Jarvis asked for the hand of the girl he is courting, Ann Cox. Her father gives his blessing and on the seventh of December next both families, of yeomen stock, will unite in Cuddington church.

Blunt like most farmers Rycharde may be, yet he has enough of the social graces expected of his yeoman rank, just below squire in the pecking order.

In fact, he has grown up in a family used to a certain refinement of living. The silver spoons already mentioned in grandfather Richard's Will are in daily use, as is the gilded goblet that recalls his father, Francis, who drank from it as head of the household. For young Rycharde, climbing as an infant into the parental bed of a morning, it had been a lesson in classical mythology to gaze up at the tester of Arras tapestry - now too worn to hang as it once did on the wall
- yet still precious enough to preserve as an heirloom of mediaeval origin.

It comes to dawn on him that these are relics from a more affluent stage of their family history.

Given that grandfather Richard had inherited from past generations - and he a child of Henry VII's reign for a start - by the time his turn came to benefit, heirlooms were rather thin on the ground. Though it had meant that by "share and share alike" goods and chattels were fairly distributed down the line.

Use of fine things engenders fine thought and use of fine words on occasion..and what better opportunity presents itself than a marriage proposal? It is an age when ordinary folk do sprinkle their language with imagery to make it more meaningful. To convey Rycharde's steadfastness - though he is unlikely to rise to the poetic vision of Henry V's declaration to Kate, I hope that Shakespeare would forgive my adapting it as if coming from the ardent young farmer himself:-

"A good heart ,Ann, is the sun and the moon; or, rather, the sun, and not the moon, for it shines bright and never changes, but keeps his course truly. If thou will have such a one, take me; and take me, take a farmer; take a farmer, take thy spouse."

Ann most certainly does - and will endeavour to make him the best of wives. For long she has spun at wool and flax, and can sew. She has helped her mother in curing and:

"Besides, I can make medecines from herbs prescribed by the doctor, whenever one of the family is ill", she says.

"And as for your cowslip wine - I can vouch for that!" laughs Rycharde.

Her elder wine was the better that year, she insists.

They shyly kiss - and he longs for the day he will be in her capable hands!

FARM BUILDINGS

A marriage has been arranged. The two families have met... the dowry proposed, her Thirds met in the contract. Thus widowhood is taken care of, heaven forbid!

It is a bonny wedding. Children, nephews and nieces, have been out early to find December roses still blooming - Ann has a nosegay after all the winter dearth of flowers. Her kirtle, fit for a bride, was sewn by her mother and the maids on the farm. It is not too chilly a day but that little cape does not come amiss for her shoulders on the trip back to the farm.

An aroma of pig roasting on the spit is wafted towards them. The wedding feast is laid in the barn at trestle tables. If the company crowd up together they'll have enough room on the benches. Rycharde's brother, Christopher, is there with his son, John, just three weeks old, and Wyborough, his daughter, still at the toddling stage. The brothers' sister, Dorothie, arrives and also Elynor, another sibling who is urging her husband, Richard Burch, to propose a toast to the couple's happiness later. So much depends, he proclaims, on a fruitful issue from the marital bed. May Ann turn out to be a good bed woman for Rycharde, is the hope of Ann herself!....Then with music from bagpipes, and on with dances of old, much merriment and affection, it reaches the climax of the proceedings when the company lead the couple to the bridal chamber and leave amid good natured laughter....but they will expect to hear in the morning if there is any evidence of conception having taken place.

The first of ten children is on the way. Let us hope there will be sons among them, but they need have no fear... The marriage proved quite fecund: out of ten children came three sons - strong yeomen farmers who lived to a ripe old age. Every daughter was married off - and with all the grandchildren as a consequence - combined to make a happy issue to my winter's tale.

LEONARD
"HARDY, BRAVE AND STRONG"

Ashendon, a tiny village perched on high, with its few cottages, looks much as it did in 1642 to our ancestor, a youthful Uncle Leonard. In company with his younger brother, Edward, he was farming an area of the Jarvis family land down below on Pollicott field. It was usual for Haddenham farmers to graze their sheep on higher ground to avoid foot rot in the likely flooding of the fields round Haddenham. Especially at lambing time, the brothers must have climbed up to worship at St. Mary's on Ashendon's narrow plateau, with its extensive views over the Buckinghamshire countryside.

Not all that far off as the crow flies, in a southerly direction, lies Wendover, where my grandparents lived in the thirties and forties on the edge of the Chilterns --Bacombe and Coombe Hills sweeping down to their garden on the Icknield Way.

Every day my grandfather used to stand at his bedroom window, to train his binoculars over a wide expanse of the county across the Vale of Aylesbury and with great enthusiasm pick out the tall chimneys of Calvert's brick kilns as proof of good visibility that day. Unconsciously he would have taken into his sights Haddenham and Ashendon, unaware that there lay our Jarvis roots. It was for me to discover in recent years.

Now, coversely, here I was on an April day in 1997, from Ashendon looking towards Wendover -- with just visible, Bacombe and Coombe Hills - and Velvet Lawn (its local name) rising from the grounds of Chequers, beloved countryside I roamed over as a child and teenager.

Behind me stood Ashendon church, which once caught the footsteps and murmers in prayer of Leonard's 17th century England. The interior has kept the simplicity of the past so poignantly evoked on a scrap of paper affixed to a pillar. Its faded writing invites the visitor to ponder the lot of those who sought sanctuary there during the troublous times of plague and war -- a reminder that Leonard and Edward must have knelt there on occasions in the period leading up to the Civil War.

Leonard was 25 in 1642, Edward 20. Both young farmers, just as their fellow Bucks countrymen, were politically aware of the grave danger to Parliament from a despotic king. That must be why the two brothers withheld their contributions when Charles I asked the populace for money to raise an army to put down the Irish rebellion.

It was suspected that he might use it against Parliament instead. Ashendon's list of subscribers is clear: Leonard and Edward took the oath of allegiance, yet gave not a penny. This was a brave act not to be underestimated - for they could have been arrested, or worse.

But they were old enough to remember the shining example of their compatriot, John Hampden, whose refusal in 1636 to pay a King's illegally imposed tax of ship-money on John's land at Stoke Manderville had championed the rights of Englishmen to be governed by Parliament and not by decree of absolute monarchy.

Now the continued political activities of Hampden, Pym and others put them in grave danger, and in January 1642 Charles entered the Commons with an armed guard to arrest the five--only to find, in his own words, that the birds had flown. Hampden's escape and triumphant return a few days later provoked a mood of excitement in Buckinghamshire, and a thousand horsemen rode into London from the county-- swearing to live and die for parliament. Whether Leonard and Edward Jarvis were

The Title-piece of a Commonwealth Newspaper. It reported parliamentary enactments and proceedings.

among them, I should love to know.

It is not known when Leonard's association with the Hampden family began. But how much they were to figure in his life comes to light in his Last Will and Testament of 1692 in which he reveals himself as "yeoman of Great Hampden". As he was not a landowner in the area - and judging from the Will itself, his intimacy with the Hampden household would make him "yeoman" in the sense of Steward or Major Domo at Hampden House, particularly as he refers to Richard Hampden (son of the Patriot) and his son, John, as "my honoured master".

Unless employed in widowhood, it seems that the staff in great houses were not expected or even allowed to marry - and Leonard appears to have been a bachelor.

It is only later that he refers to any ownership of land - in the Friarage, Aylesbury, which he had recently purchased from Sir John Pakington, whose family had held the Friarage for generations. Leonard bequeaths his land to nephew Richard Jarvis (distant grandfather of ours). Those familiar with the modern sprawl of Aylesbury will find it difficult to visualize as pastural that area above the station still called the Friarage (originally sold off at the dissolution of the monasteries).

First in a long line of beneficiaries are "Mr. Richard Hampden and Madam Letitia Hampden (sonne and daughter of my honoured Master John Hampden Esq." (and great grandchildren of the Patriot) "to each of them a guinea" which was quite a respectable sum then.

The wording of the next bequest ends on a touching personal note: "unto Mr. William Keats and Mrs. Anne Reade servants to my honoured Master Richard Hampden Esq. to each of them ten shillings of lawfull English money to buy them gloves in rememberance of me" - commemorating a mutual friendship deeply felt. Gloves were costly for their exquisite workmanship, especially the richly embroidered cuff. By savouring the pleasure of drawing them over the hand each time - the wearer could not fail to recall the donor of cherished memory.

It may have been Leonard's imposed bachelorhood that brought out a paternal feeling towards his own close relatives, for everyone of his brothers and numerous sisters, nephews and nieces get legacies on a "share and share alike" basis as he puts it. His solicitous regard for kin put me in mind of the generous spirited Jarvis relatives of the 20th century - and Leonard, across the centuries, comes over just as darling as those I have known and loved.

His parents, Richard and Elizabeth, picked an uncommon name for that time. After the fifth century Frankish saint, Leon, it confers the attributes "hardy, brave and strong". Leonard lives up to his name - especially as he had reached the good age of 74 when buried at Great Hampden on June 4th 1695.

June had been the month also of John Hampden's death, from a mortal wound at Chalgrove Field in 1642. It drew forth from the nephew of that other great Parliamentarian, John Pym, that never man lost "a truer and faithfuller friend". He might allow me to borrow this tribute as epitaph for Leonard Jarvis.

A London Trained Band Soldier, 1642-49.

JOHN HAMPDEN.

CHARLES I DEMANDS THE FIVE MEMBERS

CHARLES I.

3. SILVER POUND STRUCK AT OXFORD. 1644

"WHAT WAS IT LIKE IN THE WAR, GRANDFATHER?"

It was the second day of April 1680 and young Jarvis was on his way back from his daily lessons with the curate, shared with other Haddenham village boys who showed an aptitude for learning. One of a long line of Richards - the traditional name given to the eldest son of the eldest son born to generations of this yeoman family - no wonder he was a favourite with his grandfather. Like today, he would take the track to the old man's farm after school and invade the kitchen where grandmother Elizabeth would most likely be making cakes or biscuits - just in time to dip his finger in the mixture before it was whisked off to be cooked.

On this spring afternoon grandfather was nowhere in sight. In fact, Richard Jarvis the Elder was closetted with important matters on hand - his Last Will and Testament. For this long-living yeoman farmer, born in 1621, it was only natural to feel "fraile of bodie" just as the scribe had penned the opening phrase. Yet of "perfect mind and memory, thanks be to God".

A distant buzz of conversation heralded old Richard himself. At the sight of his grandson he beamed. " You're to get my best red bullock," he confided lovingly.

"And our other grandchildren?" asked Elizabeth...Well, each would get a lamb and a ewe when the time came.Grandmother, anticipating his quest for ale to offer the assembled company, began to take down the pewter tankards. "Let's see... how many?".. Well, there were witnesses: John Rosse, Thomas Greenwood and Thomas Bartlett... and, of course, the executors - "the loving sonnes": John ,Thomas - and Richard junior, young Richard's father - the lad would be riding pillion back to their farm at Kingsey in a while. "Ale for six ,then - oh, and the scribe - and you, husband, of course!"

"It was lucky," mused the old man, watching her fill up from the keg, "That the military did not find our plate when they came nosing round."

"Oh, don't bring up the war!" said Elizabeth, "That was years ago!"

But young Richard loved to hear again and again his grandparents' tales of the great rebellion - and what life was like in the Buckinghamshire countryside as newly weds in 1643, one year into the conflict.

Garrisions of Royalists and opposing Parliamentarians sprang up all over the county,

A Dragoon or Mounted Infantryman, trained and armed to fight either on horseback or on foot, 1642-49.

and with the King's men in Haddenham itself, and Roundheads in Aylesbury nearby - there was much activity. Both sides plundered grain, horses and cattle and anything else of value. The Jarvis yeomen, like all the rest, stowed their provisions and livestock away out of sight wherever possible.

"Tell me again how you hid the bacon!" And the expectant boy clapped at the familiar reply: "Down the well." He would have loved to outwit the marauding soldiers. "And then we'd turf it over," added Elizabeth, "You couldn't tell there was a hole in the ground at all."

"Did anyone ever fall through?" her grandson asked.

"Sometimes a farm labourer forgot; then it was all hands to get him out."

"Did the soldiers surprise you?"

"Grandfather and I would take it in turns to keep watch. When the family were at table usually. If we gave the alarm all the food had to go back in the hidey holes - and we had to make haste!" But it wasn't a laughing matter then. Your crops could be despoiled out of pure spite. And it didn't matter which side you were on.

"There was no love lost between us and the military," Elizabeth said grimly. "But everyone was in the same boat. My kinsmen, the Platers suffered too."

"We didn't quarrel among ourselves like some families," grandfather was happy to say. "In the long run good fortune did prevail."

And Elizabeth bestowed a loving glance in young Richard's direction. "God has smiled kindly on us," she said.

N.B. In Richard's Last Will and Testament of 1680 he mentions the names of the acres and roods of land he bequeaths in the open fields of Haddenham: they are Rumpitts, Stoarten, Honey Furlong, Strandway by Cuddington Brook, and so on......

FREEZING WINTER

It must be remembered that until the 1750s New Year fell in March. The December and early months of 1739/40 were hit by the Big Freeze, when the Thames froze over and the ice was thick enough to support a fair, known as the Thames Frost Fair. Booths were constructed of the oars and sails of the boats - normally plying on the river, London's main highway then. The Frost Fair of 1740 was one of several in the river's history but more spectacular than most. In those days old London Bridge with its multiple arches slowed down the river flow which made it conducive to freezing up, and there was very little oil on the water - if any.

All over the country lakes and ponds and rivers bore skaters, sledges and an assortment of pastimes: for instance, villagers with putting sticks might play a kind of ice golf like in the paintings of Avercamp and other Flemish masters over the water. The good folk of Haddenham must have joined in the fun.

The Thames Frost Fair, 1740 - painting in oils by the author; exhibited at the Royal Academy in 1953, in Brussels 1970, and now in a private collection in Belgium. (Dimension 4'6" x 3'3"; signed Gloria Jarvis). At that time the painter was lecturer on historic costume at the Polytechnic School of Art, Regent Street, London.

Mary Jarvis must have gone to a tailor in Aylesbury.
This print is just the right period for Mary's wardrobe.

A LADY'S WARDROBE 1735

When Richard II invented the handkerchief he had no idea how prized an asset it was to become by the 18th and 19th centuries. Of silk, no fashionable toilet was complete without one. It was expensive enough for Moll Flanders to risk her liberty stealing for--- and remember Fagin drooling over his collection filched by the Artful Dodger from the pockets of the unwary!

A handkerchief was so important an item as to be mentioned in one's Will--- like Mary Jarvis's of 1735. I should love to ask that distant great-grandmother of mine if those precious handkerchiefs were ever used for practical purposes, such as blowing one's nose. But most likely "my best silk handkerchief" bequeathed to her son, Richard, would have been a costume accessory only, to overhang a pocket or be daintily held in the hand as a status symbol when doing the social round of Haddenham and its environs.

While on the subject of her Will, Mary Jarvis allows a glimpse into a wardrobe that befitted a comfortably off farmer's wife, with obviously some pretensions to fashion. Waddesdon born, daughter of yeoman Thomas Wiggins (the name is of Breton origin, whose bearers in the mists of time were followers of William the Conqueror) Mary married yeoman Richard Jarvis of Haddenham in 1696, and out lived him by two years. Had he, I wonder, ever taken a dutiful husbandly interest in her clothes, such as, "my black and white crape gown...my lightest coloured crape gown...my black damas quilted coat lined with a check... my black scarf, and my shifts...aprons...head clothes"---an apron, at that time, was a decorative accessory---and frilled caps were worn not only at home, but under one's hat (usually with the brim up as a tricorne) when sallying forth. If of straw, the hat had a ribbon over the crown and tied under the chin, thus pinching the brim against the face---a style later revived in the 1870s, and known as a "Dolly Varden" in its association with a Dicken's novel.

Were some of these garments made by Mary herself? Or was there a proverbial little dressmaker in Haddenham or Aylesbury? Mary may have woven "the lining of homemade stuff" of a further "black quilted coat" mentioned.

As to her cherished handkerchiefs, they were bought, perhaps, from a pedlar passing through the countryside, resigned, no doubt, to having his high prices haggled over.

One thing's for sure: whenever Mary walked abroad in Haddenham, her feet must have been thrust into overshoes or pattens against the muddy highway and ruts, Did anything like a pony and trap exist in those days?

A gentleman of William III's reign. A compromise between Cavalier extravagance and Puritan simplicity.

A gentleman of Anne's reign. Note the development of the wig.

Fire Engine.

A Hackney Coachman.

a Taylor

The Stocks and Pillory. A severe mode of punishment in that prisoners were open to public ill-treatment.

A Part of the 18th Century

The other day I came across my costume designs for the production at the Theatre des Beaux Arts, Brussels, of "She Stoops to Conquer" by Oliver Goldsmith. "Why not add a few to illustrate this family history?" I thought, "To give a flavour of the mid-18th century - and the shape of the kind of clothes there might be in the family wardrobe." Here are some of them, with a few servants thrown in for good measure.

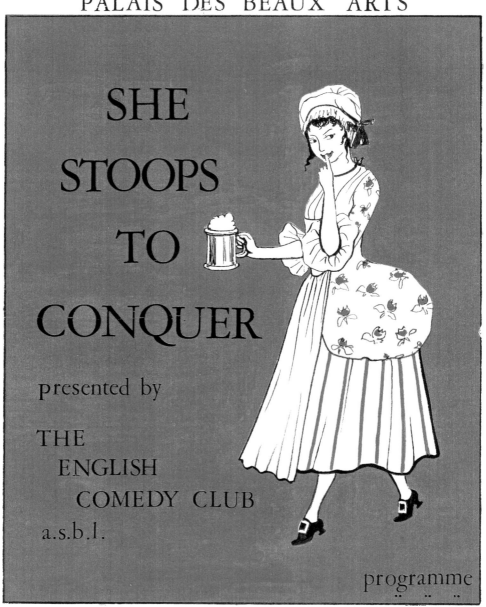

SHE
STOOPS
TO
CONQUER

presented by

THE
ENGLISH
COMEDY CLUB
a.s.b.l.

programme

price **15** fr.

"She Stoops to Conquer"

Grey black bow
and neck ribbon
with pink bow at nape

Fichu tucked in

black ribbon
round wrist

Kate Hardcastle   (alternative)

33

"She Stoops to Conquer"

Kate Hardcastle — her "housewife's dress".

"She Stoops to Conquer"

Old style wig

Old style frock coat
with skirt

Mr. Hardcastle.

"She Stoops to Conquer"

Tony Lumpkin

"great flaxen wig" (older style)

"All I can say will not
ague down a single
button from his
clothes" - (Mrs H.)

Mr. Hardcastle - older style frock coat (1740) "I like the
things"

"She Stoops to Conquer"

Chemise
full

blacked out
teeth

apron

farm labourer or servant

"She Stoops to Conquer"

Panniers
with Watteau
like back

apron for decoration

Constance

39

"She Stoops to Conquer"

Smock

sabots

Roger, a servant:
First Fellow

40

Wig,

Patches on face.

Shawl-type fichu caught ~~up~~ with black bow.

Ruffles at elbow.

Mrs. Handcastle. Silk dress over Panniers Taffeta apron.

Waistcoat with
sleeves too short.
Stockings wrinkled
with big holes at
heels.
Shoes too big.

1st Servant

Same hat as
for First Fellow
with brim
buttoned up to
crown to form
tricorne.

Neckerchief

Shirt with
sleeves too long
& hole at
elbow

Sash
Sleeveless
waistcoat.
Breeches.

Stockings and
cloggs as for
First Fellow.

2nd Servant.

43

"She Stoops to Conquer"

Maid

"She Stoops to Conquer"

Hastings

Cloak of
nylon a similar
mat.
"Slime" painted on.

Cloak with a
large tear on right
side — dragging a
branch caught up
in the material.

Hat with
feathers.

branch
attached
to dress.

Mrs. Hardcastle, muddied
and bedraggled from
the pond.

46

"She Stoops to Conquer"

Black
hat,
wig
Boots &
shoes,
off white
stockings
Ruffled shirt
Cravat
Ruffles at
wrist

Marlow

47

My grandmother, Emily Jarvis, in her enchanting garden at Wendover in the 1930s. Born in 1858, she was a forward looking Victorian. In running away from home to get a job and lead an independent life, she gave an early indication of Women's Lib.

Val Jarvis. They met in the draper's he eventually bought.

"THIS MONSTROUS REGIMENT OF GRANDMOTHERS"

John Knox's "monstrous phrase"* thundering from the pulpit, though directed primarily at Mary Queen of Scots, would appear to be taking in most of womankind. In which case, Knox, quite unwittingly, was condemning his own ancestral grandmothers stretching back in time. But then any part heredity played had not yet surfaced in 16th century minds, so the preacher had no idea how much the genes of these good ladies had contributed to his indomitable makeup.

For the rest of our particular Jarvis folk - courtship of ancestral great-grandmothers by Jarvis yeomen enriched the family tree with manifold new branches.

Here comes the bride...daughters of yeomen themselves...an Ann Cox twice in the line...and one of each of Elizabeth Plater, Martha Meere, Susan Scrivener of Leighton Buzzard...not forgetting capable Elizabeth Bonnyck. She took over the Falcon inn at Great Brickhill on the death of her husband, Thomas Peppiatt, landlord, cattle farmer and butcher. He died in 1726.

Their son, William, a sheep farmer, took for wife Susan Scrivener, who died in 1740 giving birth to their second son, Scrivener. Their first born, John Peppiatt, married a yeoman's lass with the lovely name of Damaris. Among their many offspring it was daughter, Ann Peppiatt, who in 1793 wed William Jarvis, baker of Luton. A year later son, Thomas, was born, destined to marry in 1824 Hannah Adkin. This event brought my great- great grandfather, Thomas, into the Durrant family, for his wife, Hannah, was the daughter of Ann Durrant and John Adkin of Billington, farmer. Ann's father was Francis Durrant, the bailiff on the Liscomb estate, Soulbury, which he farmed as well as his own dairy farm at Great Brickhill. The Lovetts of Liscomb erected a plaque to his memory in All Saints, Soulbury, together with that of his son, Thomas Durrant, who suceeded his father as bailiff on the estate.

The nature of a dearly departed can shine through the wording of a Will as when Mary Jarvis, nee Wiggins, arrayed her fashionable garments in 1735. But it was her "best silk handkerdhief" that marked her as a fashion conscious lady. Most of all, I find Mary's tender regard for her brother-in-law, John Jarvis, "my beloved and trusty friend", touching in it's sentiment, and an eloquent way of appointing him overseer of her Last Will and Testament.

* Knox said: "This monstrous regiment of women".

John Knox's diatribe against the female sex four centuries ago might have an echo today from some quarters, against the excesses of Women's Lib. But without our bevy of past grandams we would not be what we are. For their traits of character helped mould us - even though we can only glimpse them through the mists of time.

Mary Jarvis, nee Wiggins, after a succession of three daughters, was blest with a son - baptised Richard, of course, being the first male. He grew up to be a yeoman of Cuddington. His wife, whom we only know as Ann, would have worn this style of dress at the time they were wed, which must have been the late 1730s, because in 1740 their first son - yet another Richard - was born.

Townsend, Haddenham, with one of the Jarvis farms on the left, was the part where the nonconformists congregated.   (Photo Anne Jarvis)

"USING THEIR LOAF"

Within the natural progression of wheat--into grain--into flour--into bread--the means of livelihood among our recent forebears shifts from husbandry to bakery. When, towards the end of the 18th century, tilling of the land was no longer viable for as many Jarvis sons as before, they began to set themselves up as bakers, so that during the 19th century they spread to Great Brickhill, Soulbury, Aylesbury and Luton. And with a Jarvis corn-factor in Haddenham even the purchase of bread's staple ingredient could be "kept in the family", the source being, no doubt, relatives still farming roundabout. To coin a popular phrase--these newcomers to trade were "using their loaf", for bread, fundamental to life, in filling a universal need ensured a steady livelihood. Besides, this end product, bread, was a vital link with the land--a feeling strongly felt in the bones of these farmers' sons and grandsons. As bakers, they might unconsciously see themselves at their ovens as still part of their agricultural heritage.

Records show the following Jarvis bakers: William Jarvis, who married Elizabeth Clements of Great Brickhill (marriage bonds and allegations, 31st May, 1794); Thomas Jarvis, recorded as baker in 1842 and 1853 in Cambridge street, Aylesbury (his Will mentions copyhold cottages in Haddenham) ; John Dover Jarvis was a baker in Haddenham; in the 1830s; while our three grandfathers in succession--William, baker at Luton, must have taught the trade to his son, Thomas of Soulbury--and Frederick, his son, worked in his father's bakery before setting up as Master Baker at 16 Brittania Street, Aylesbury.

It seems that as husbandry dwindled so the perpetuation of Richards and Johns at the baptismal font gave way to a freedom of choice of names, following the trend of the 19th century. Thus ended hundreds of years of tradition.

A Dame School in the early 19th century.

All Saints, Soulbury (photo Anne Jarvis)

BOND OF INDEMNITY

Whatever happened to Ulialia - Ulialia Sewell - after 1802, the year she brought a paternity action against Thomas Jarvis? He was the eldest of the twelve children of my great-great-great-great grandfather, Richard Jarvis, husbandman of Hollingdon in the parish of Soulbury, north-east Bucks.

If all went well at the lying -in, then the result of Uncle Thomas's indiscretion, so long ago, will have given me another distant cousin to notch up on the family tree - albeit the other side of the blanket.

The wronged woman was bold enough to have a Bond of Indemnity served on Thomas, by this time already courting another, in all probability the one he was to marry two years later, in 1804. But "boys will be boys", might have shrugged his intended, Phoebe Read, if a breath of Ulialia ever came to her ears.

Father, of course, paid up, at the demand of the Overseers of the Poor. Who knows what family scenes took place? Yet his wrath might have been tempered with indulgence - seeing that Thomas was the least favoured, not having been set up in trade like his brothers, but was employed as a servant (at Linslade). No doubt, his copperplate handwriting was put to good use by his employer (who, ironically, might have been illiterate, like so many, still, at that time).

And Ulialia? "Sounds like a theatrical family," observed Eve*, "No farm labourer would have thought of a name like that!" The Bond of Indemnity describes her as "singlewoman" whose child on the way was "likely to be born a bastard" - Thomas, then , had made it quite clear he would not be taking her to the altar. His father, Richard, as a respected member of the community, could have well done without any notoriety - let alone expense - that his son's peccadillo created. The one with the money bags, he submitted to being bound with Thomas to the Churchwardens of Gt. Brickhill (Ulialia's parish) who exacted a tidy sum for those days: £40, to cover the birth, maintenance , education, and upbringing of the child about to come into the world.

I wonder what fanciful name Ulialia put forward at the baptism? She proved a woman of decision. As for Thomas - did he ever wonder if the infant's features resembled some other man's. Coming up to his fortieth year, he could not have been so naive not to ask himself: "Is the child a Jarvis, after all?"

* Eve McLaughlin, historian and genealogist

Great-grandparents, John Henry
Eschmann (Swiss imigré) and
Sarah Ann Hawkins, parents of
Emily Jarvis; Sarah Ann died
when Emily was an infant.

THE VICTORIANS

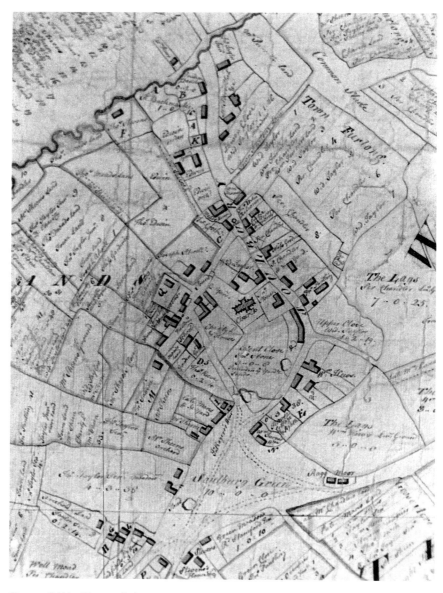

Part of "A Plan of the Manor of Soulbury situate in Buckinghamshire belonging to Jonathan Lovett Esq., Surveyd and Pland in the Year 1769 by Wm Woodward".   (Photo Anne Jarvis)

Courtesy of the Centre for Buckinghamhire Studies

THOMAS JARVIS

1794 - 1880

When his grandchildren quarrelled (as children do)
he would wag his finger and say:
"Fie, fie! 'Tis dog's delight to bark and bite!"

All Saints, Soulbury (photo Anne Jarvis)

Thomas Jarvis toughened it out through four reigns. And life was hard in the 19th century. His grandfather, yeoman Richard Jarvis, left the family farm in his Will to his son, Robert, in the parish of Soulbury at Hollingdon. Thomas was also a beneficiary in Richard's Will - to the tune of five guineas on coming of age - worth much more in those days. Richard's second son, William, born in 1764, was Thomas's father, who went off to Luton to become a baker. In 1793 he obtained a licence to marry Anne Peppiatt, herself a farmer's daughter, of Great Brickhill and Leighton Buzzard, and the following year Thomas was born. His grandfather Richard's farm, handed on to Uncle Robert Jarvis in 1811, was the last in the family line - it was then inherited by his daughter, Elizabeth, and her husband Thomas Deverell of Ewell, Oxford, and the effects shared by James Mead of Stewkley, Bucks, both farmers, in 1851. Agriculture in our direct line from mediaeval times had ended.

Thomas Jarvis (1794 - 1880), started life as a school-master in Harpenden, Hertforshire, then settled in Soulbury, Buckinghamshire, as baker, parish clerk and postmaster.

Peter Jarvis, my cousin once removed, and, like me, descended in direct line from Thomas Jarvis - seen here with his wife, Nichola (Nikki), and one of their two sons, James and Charles. Thomas, passing on the same facial features, must have resembled Peter as a young man.

My own grandpa's memory of his grandfather, the above Thomas Jarvis, came vividly to life as I coaxed it out of him long ago in 1940. Still a schoolgirl then, I had begun to get curious about past kith and kin. Apparently, in their Victorian childhood grandpa and his little sister, Eliza, loved to stay with their grandfather, Thomas, in Soulbury, a pretty village in north-east Buckinghamshire. Parents, Frederick and Jane Ellen, forbade them travelling from Aylesbury in wet weather on the fell-monger's cart, their only means of transport. Once, when the sky was overcast on the eve of departure, the two little ones stole upstairs to kneel at their bedside and "pray God, not to let it rain so that they could go to grandad's". Lake, the fell-monger, would call for them at 3 o'clock of a Saturday, having sold his skins at Aylesbury market. After pocketing a tip from Frederick, Lake would set off with his charges to Soulbury to deposit them at 24 The Green, opposite the blacksmith's forge and where the children loved to play round the pond. A shout to Thomas from Lake, brought him bustling out, smiling benevolence, in frockcoat, knee-length fustian breeches and gaiters - no need for his beaver hat. Lifting the children down, he pressed them lovingly to him. Following on his heels, the two aunts gave a kiss, Sarah ever kind - Hannah, too, "in her grim cold way". Grandmother, confined to her invalid bed, raised herself up to greet them - in the evening loving to listen to the children's hymn singing at her bedside.

They would rise at dawn and if it were winter dress by candlelight. If Thomas had baked some rolls they had them hot for breakfast, with boiled eggs and sometimes beef. Then Val accompanied him on his rounds in the pony and trap to deliver bread in the village and to the Lovetts at Liscomb.

There must have still been the flavour of a lingering 18th century about Soulbury and the surrounding countryside reminiscent of a Gainsborough landscape; including the inhabitants, most of whom couldn't write. In fact Thomas was in demand, especially for composing love letters - billets doux. His father, William, and grandfather, Richard, were also literate; but I notice that in going as far back as the 17th century Jarvis Wills, quite a few of the men could write - or at least sign in a tolerable hand.

There were tea parties, where once Miss Durrant caused a sensation in her crinoline of shot silk. This impressed Val - and the little boy grew up to be a draper; significantly, he had an appreciation of materials at an early age.

Boyishly, he would swing on the bell ropes in All Saints, Soulbury - getting carried up into the tower one day, to the consternation of his grandfather, who danced about in agitation below.

I have a lasting affection for Thomas - and of course, for Val who inherited his intense blue eyes and in the same way, "looked you straight in the eye". Thomas Jarvis lived through the reigns of George III, George IV, William IV and Victoria. His talent for writing enabled him to earn a living. It gave him a start in life as a schoolmaster in Harpenden - until the National Schools came in; although the parents still had to pay whatever they could afford, the church that was behind the new educational enterprise was able to provide more resources - and Thomas's pupils melted away. After a spell as an agricultural labourer on his Uncle Robert's farm at Hollingdon, he became Parish Clerk, and was responsible for the Census when it came round. But as sub-postmaster in the village of Soulbury he was invaluable - it was another string to his bow which he combined with his bakery.

The crinoline, when it reached its apex in the 1860s, must have been a talking point in a small community like Soulbury's. Thomas's daughters, Sarah and Hannah, were both dressmakers based at home. To reach any sophistication in design they probably consulted a ladies' magazine, produced in bound volumes of hand tinted engravings of what were then fashion drawings, to be bought from book shops in Leighton Buzzard or Aylesbury. If the client supplied the steel frame, then draping the skirt over it was a practice perfected by experience. Presumably the client also

provided the material, Sarah and Hannah simple trimmings. Of course, the finished model would be a scaled down version of London's or Paris's!

Thomas probably taught his children the rudiments of reading and writing - Val, on his visits, certainly profitted from his coaching in copperplate (he always said).

The reason why some of our Jarvis yeomen in past centuries were literate while others were not depended on a boy's aptitude to learn. If he showed signs his father sent him to whatever passed for the village school - often a small circle run by the curate. Otherwise, a son was left to follow his own bent in pursuing a living.

Wesleyan Chapel, Soulbury (Photo Anne Jarvis).

THOMAS'S FAMILY

Thomas and Hannah Jarvis were Wesleyans, and their first born, Ann Durrant Jarvis, was christened at Eaton Bray Wesleyan Chapel on 13th April 1825 - and on the same day at All Saints, Soulbury; at that date nonconformists were permitted to be baptised in chapel as long as they agreed to go through the ceremony in the parish church. By the time Sarah was christened in 1827 a Wesleyan chapel had been built in Soulbury, where she and the rest of the family were baptised: Charles in 1829, Frederick in 1831, Hannah in 1833, Mary the next year, Eliza in 1839. Charles was to become a storekeeper in Swanbourne; Frederick worked with his father in the bakery, and eventually set up on his own in Britannia Street, Aylesbury. There was another boy, William, who died young, but survived his schooldays. In the 1841 Census Ann Durrant pops up again as a housemaid of sixteen in the Lovett household at Liscomb. No doubt she saw to it to be often in the kitchen when her father delivered the bread, a daily occurrence.

According to the Census of 1851 Eliza, already 12, was a lodger at Susannah Gurney's, number 10 The Green, Soulbury; schoolmistress for plaiting straw, who had half a dozen boarders as pupils. Later this skill earned Eliza a living sewing straw hats in the centre of the industry at Luton. Tragically, in her forties, misfortune overtook her, for the 1881 Census for Luton Workhouse shows her as inmate with a two month old illegitimate son. It was her only means of subsistence, for, according to the harsh times, she had brought disgrace on her family and could not expect any help from them. But I wonder if they even knew - whether she deliberately kept it from them. Eliza's father, Thomas, had died in January, the previous year. I cannot think he would have been so heartless as to deny her shelter with the babe, his own grandson, however shameful. But a sister was another matter - and Hannah, the only one mentioned in the Soulbury Census as living at home, would have been too primly sensitive - let alone censorious, to withstand the scandal.

It is poignant that Eliza had chosen to name her son after her brother, Frederick - a nostalgic reminder of family and home and happier days.

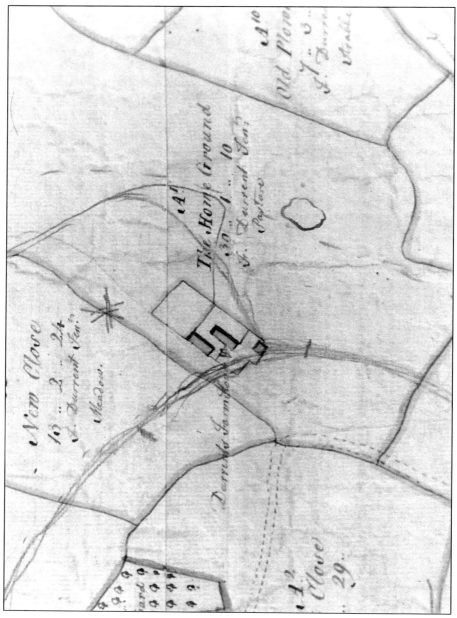

(4 x great-grandfather) Francis Durrent's farmhouse on the Liscomb estate, Soulbury, where he was bailiff in the 18th century.

(Photo Anne Jarvis)

Courtesy of the Centre for Buckinghamhire Studies

FRED JARVIS

MINING PIONEER

LOUISE FOOTE

KOOTENAY/BOUNDARY

NATURAL-HIGH COUNTRY

Steep snow-mantled mountains in all directions. Serene deep-blue lakes once churned by stern-wheelers, now only stirred by the slap of a canoe paddle or the swirl and ker-plop of a surface-breaking trout. Forest-covered hills and emerald valleys abounding with deer. Meandering streams, rollicking rivers, steaming hot springs, and ravenous rapids. Ghost towns, historic silver- and gold-mining towns, small, friendly cities combining the best of the old and the new, and tucked-away communities of inspired artists and outdoor adventurers. These are the crisp, clean images of beautiful Kootenay Country. Hike, canoe, ski, renew. Stay a couple of weeks and you may stay a lifetime!

The first settlers came to the Kootenays in the late 1800s in search of precious metals—silver, lead, and zinc, all of which they found in large quantities—but they stayed for the bountiful harvests and scenic beauty. Located west of the Rocky Mountain region in the southeastern corner of B.C., Kootenay Country is separated into a couple of north-south valleys and small pockets of civilization by the mighty **Purcell, Selkirk,** and **Monashee** mountain ranges. In the lush green valleys lie long, narrow **Kootenay Lake,** equally long and even narrower **Upper** and **Lower Arrow** lakes, and several smaller lakes. With its almost completely mountainous terrain, this region certainly receives its share of annual precipitation, with plenty of snow (the skiing is terrific), plus a large diurnal temperature range. No boring, predictable weather on this part of the globe!

Almost all the outdoor activities in the Kootenays and Boundary Country include water in two out of its three forms. Fishing for trout, char, kokanee salmon, and freshwater cod and bass; canoeing; and skiing are the favorites. One of the most popular canoe routes focuses on Upper and Lower Arrow lakes, flanked by the Selkirk and Monashee mountains. Together these two interconnected lakes, lined with beaches and camping spots, stretch for a total of about 185 km (facilities are sparse—carry everything you need).

From a latter-day guide book.

FREDERICK WILLIAM JARVIS
MINING PIONEER OF NELSON, CANADA

Frederick William Jarvis was the eldest brother to my grandfather, Valentine Harry, and hence my great-uncle. I was familiar with his venerable face from a studio photograph on the mantle piece of my grandfather's bedroom. He had cut himself off from his family when a mere teenager to emigrate to Canada, and only got in touch with them when he was quite an old man. At long last he had felt a certain nostalgia.

In the early 1870s, when about eighteen he had signed up at the emigration office in Kingsbury Square, Aylesbury, forever as it turned out - but keeping it close to his chest, He knew that as soon as it got to the ears of his parents he would be under a severe cloud - yes, he had "got a young girl into trouble". The consequence of young love. They lived back to back - she in Cambridge Street, he in Britannia Street, enabling them to communicate via their gardens. But she was a mere housemaid - not considered of any social standing in those days.

The émigré was in his eighties when my grandfather received a letter from him about his experiences in Canada. After he died in 1942 someone sent a newspaper article about him and his long life - he died at eighty seven.

Extracts from the Nelson Daily News of March 12th and 17th of 1942 tell his Canadian story.

Fred Jarvis, Mining Pioneer

Nelson Daily News, March 12th and 17th 1942

Following are notes told to R. G. Joy, Historian of the Old Timers' Association by the late Fred Jarvis, who came to Nelson in the year 1890:   It was only after several visits to Fred's home on High Street that Mr. Joy could induce him to talk.   The following is his story:

50 PEOPLE HERE

"I was born in Aylesbury, Bucks, England, in the year 1855, came to Canada in 1873.   Was for a time in Nelson 1890, about fifty people here.

The Silver King Mine was located about 1887.   No doubt the location of this mine was the cause of Nelson being founded and later becoming the metropolis of the Kootenays. I remember Marks and Van Ness,   Kootenay Johnson,   Silver King Johnson.   I knew John Blomburg when he ran the Victoria Hotel at Ainsworth with his partner McNeil.   Porcupine Billy was quite a character.   A pioneer packer,   he had a horse that could walk a log with a good size pack.   George Johnstone was the first Customs Officer. I also knew Doc McFarlane whose brother was a banker at Beddington on the Thames, England. You remember we got sufficent money together to send him to England to undergo a serious operation. The old timers subsibed both in money and other ways,   for instance, if you were short of cash you put in some article that could be sold.

Tom Ward tried to get in touch with him   later,   but   failed.

"I also knew Joe Wilson," said Jarvis, 'the founder of the P. Burns & Co. meat business,   also Clarke, who weighed the meat at Sproats' Landing.   This meat was for the various construction camps in the country.   Joe   Wilson's transportation was by pack horses, mostly cayuse. I remember Buchanan coming to open a branch for the Bank of Montreal.   His assistant was Craig.   Applewaites office was in the building that was used for a paint shop on Josephine Street.

HAD CLAIMS

"I owned some claims near the Silver King,   in partnership with the late Billy Ward of Procter. Later, I worked for Mr. Stone, who had the contract for diamond drilling the Silver King Group, for the Hall Mines Co. in the years 1894 to 1896.   I operated a row boat called the Lady of the Lake, taking freight   and   passengers   between Queen's bay and Ainsworth,   this was before the advent of Mud Hen Davis of Mud Hen Steamboat fame.

"Gilbert Malcolm Sproat was Magistrate for the whole of the Kootenays.   He was appointed by the Court of Queen's Bench,   London,   England.   Did you know Mrs. Mcleod who had the first milk ranch in Nelson?   In the hot weather she peddled milk,   disdaining shoes and stockings.   Her first locator of land for fruit growing purposes at or near Willow Point. Busk was the next. He located at Balfour. We asked them where they thought they could sell the fruit. Young Bob McLeod was only a kid in short pants then. Now he is a Real Estate agent in one of the large cities on the Pacific Coast. He has at times been very sucessful. he was a good poker player at an early age.

"Giffin was Mining Recorder before Fitzstubbs, and acted as constable and general upholder of the law. The site of John Ward's tent was in the middle of the street that is now known as Ward Street in front of where the Hume Hotel now stands. Another constable was Benjamin Henry Lee who was an ex-captain of Marines. He in later years joined the Strathcona horse and fought in South Africa. He met his death some say, when he was lightng his pipe and a shot from a dum dum bullet tore his breast. His comrades tried to put him on a horse, but he could not manage it. Lee said: I'll pass out, you look after yourselves.' There are several stories about B. H. Lee. There was a lady, coloured, who weighed about 225 pounds. She was the worse for liquor and Lee found it difficult in landing her in jail. He threw her dress over her head and trying to pack her as one would a sack, managed to get her in the lockup. On the way he was reprimanded by a little Englishman for ill treating the lady. Lee was a man that stood over six feet, a raw-boned Marine.

"H. Selous soon after arriving went into the real estate business.

Mike Keeley and G. M. Sproat laid out Baker and Vernon Streets with a rope as no chain was to be had. Mike Keeley was a wonderful axeman and later was chairman for A. S. Farwell, the Surveyor. Claud Hamber was another real estate man, his partner's name was Thin. Hamber and Thin lived on Victoria Street near Monty Davis' residence which was on the corner where J. Blomburg's residence now stands.

Fred Jarvis, widely known as a district old timer, particulary among mining men, died at Kootenay Lake General Hospital Wednesday, aged 87.

Mr. Jarvis who had not been feeling well, was found by a neighbour, W. A. Bennett, trying to bring in a scuttle of coal while doing this. Wednesday morning he said he was feeling better, but added that during the night, going to the kitchen for a glass of water, he had fainted. Later Wednesday morning he was removed to Kootenay Lake General Hospital and died during the afternoon.

A brother in England is, as far as is known, his only surviving relative.

Mr. Jarvis who was from Buckinghamshire, England, lived in Ontario for a time when he first came to Canada, but travelled West to the Kootenays in the early days.

A SAILBOAT FERRY

At one time he operated a sailboat ferry service between Riondel and Nelson, charging $3 per trip.

He was a diamond driller, and worked at the Silver King near Nelson, and the Stemwinder in the Pheonix camp. He was in the Slocan in the early days.

It is understood he owned several claims in the Slocan and Sheep Creek districts, and he held shares in a number of big Canadian dividend-paying mines.

For many years he was a bartender in Nelson, working at the Office Saloon and later at the Hume bar, over 2 years ago. He then entered the customs and inland revenue service at Nelson, retiring on superannuation 10 or 12 years ago.

Nelson Pioneer Is Laid at Rest

Frederick William Jarvis, who first saw Nelson in 1890, was laid at rest in Nelson Memorial Park Monday afternoon. Funeral services were conducted at St. Saviour's Cathedral and at the graveside by Ven. Archdeacon Fred H. Graham.

God of the Living was the hymn sung.

Pallbearers were M. E. Harper, Martin Robicaud, Fred Irvine, W. A. Bennett, H. B. Gore, and Bud Stevens. Interment was in the Anglican plot.

Mr. Jarvis died here Wednesday.

Nelson now.

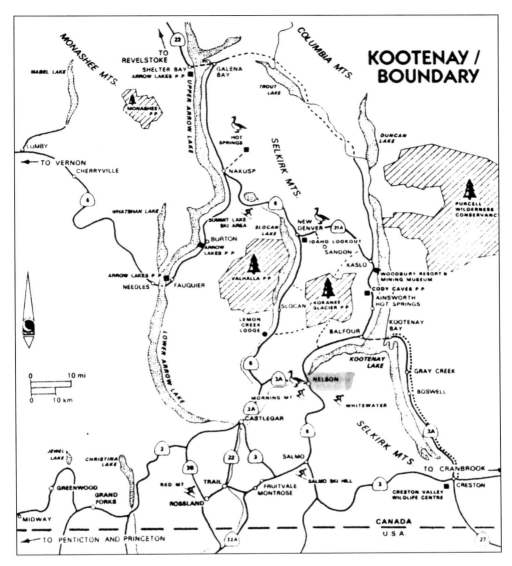

Map of the Kootenay area.

James Jarvis, Master Tailor of
Aylesbury, 1857-1899

Frederick Jarvis, Master Baker, 1831-1925
of 16 Britannia Street, Aylesbury.

Valentine Harry Jarvis, 1863-1949,
Draper, singer and director of
music in Aylesbury; his business
was at 15 High Street.

Eliza Jarvis, wife of Fred. Wm.
Jenns, of Buckingham Street,
Aylesbury, furniture makers and
retailers.

Kelly's Directory 1935

Jarvis Valentine Harry

THE SEQUEL

In recent years Frederick William's descendant paid a visit to the County Record Office in Aylesbury to try to trace him and found her long lost great-grandfather sitting in my family tree. She noted my address and got in touch with me.

One morning a postcard dropped on my mat - to give me the suprising news that I had acquired a distant cousin. Before I could get to the phone to dial her number, it rang. The voice barely concealed its excitement; there was a slight note of trepidation, too - but I was as delighted as she, the great-great grandchild of the girl made pregnant by Frederick William.

The child had been a boy, and as he grew up he cherished thoughts of tracing his father whom the family suspected of emigrating. So he joined the navy to enable him to travel and make enquiries. Unhappily, Canada was the only country he never tried.

When this new cousin of mine came to tea I was at least able to give her snaps of Frederick's brother and sister as there was a strong family likeness. She eventually paid a visit to Nelson, British Colombia - and was quite fêted. Memories of Fred and those early pioneers live on.

Three of the children of Frederick Jarvis senior, with a very indistinct one of himself, but have no better. He followed his father,Thomas into the bakery at Soulbury - then set up on his own in Aylesbury. His eldest, Frederick William, in turn, assisted him until he left for Canada in the 1870s. (Photos opposite page)

Frederick William worked in the bakery that was on the ground floor of the central building in Toronto on his arrival in Canada, 1873.

Grandpa Val Jarvis

VAL SPARKS OFF HARMONY IN AYLESBURY

It is more than likely that a man born on St. Valentine's day will be baptised with that name. And so it was with my grandfather, Valentine Harry. A Victorian, yet one who moved with the times, his was an Aylesbury family, quite unaware of its long line of of Jarvis forebears with roots in the Bucks countryside as yeomen up to the early 19th century. That would be for me to discover.

Educated at the Grammer School in the 1860s in its old building by St. Mary's Church - at a time when a pupil who did not take sufficient pains over his copperplate script would have his knuckles rapped by the master's steel ruler - the boy little realised one day he would be Vice Chairman of the governors.

My memories of him are vivid and warm. As a child I was too shy to follow my impulse and throw my arms around his kneck - he was so huggable. Instead as I grew up I expressed my affection in countless drawings of him. His white hair, keen blue eyes, pink cheeks were so pictorial. Many's the time I sketched him in his armchair - reading or dropping off into a snooze or as I followed him round the garden on a weeding foray, stabbing at dandelions with his weed gun. Grandpa taking breakfast in bed was a favourite topic of mine. This octogenarian once posed a whole quarter of an hour holding a heavy breakfast cup to his lips - till quietly came: "You must tell me when you want to stop." What a lovely way of saying he'd had enough!

In his younger days he had been a singer. That is, outside his business as a draper and ladies' outfitter at 15 High Street, Aylesbury. In 1881 his fine tenor voice had won him an appointment at Christ Church, Oxford. But as a career he felt the stipend would not be enough in the event of supporting a family.

However, music remained an important love of his life, leading to his being secretary and conductor to the Vale of Aylesbury Harmonic Society, and from 1900 to 1911 choir master of St. John's Church, having first laid the foundation of the choir. It was in those years that business took him all over the county by pony and trap. On the road he would often encounter a countryman called John North whose eccentricity and pithy sayings earned him a place in legend as the Dickensian character he could have been. In fact his fame lived on to the 1940s to merit an article about him in the journal The Countryman.

John also loved music - and would frequently cry "halt!" to my grandfather at the roadside while he tested him with some technical questions on musical notation. One day grandpa gave him a complimentary ticket for the Messiah that he was to conduct at St. John's. He sat spellbound in the front row. Afterwards, when asked by my grandfather what he thought of the performance, he spelt out his verdict in personal style: "There weren't a pin's point 'twixt what it was and what it ought to be!"

Over the years my visits to grandfather's grave have been taken up more and more with the struggle against the grass obliterating the last line on the headstone: "He liked to sing thy praises" - which is worth saving as a fitting epitaph for one whose heart was in music, and who, happily, rests in the lee of the Chilterns in Wendover churchyard. The wind in the trees might be said to whisper a refrain.

Sketch in conté crayon lined up to transfer to canvas and the subsequent oil painting

On the day I asked grandpa to remember his grandfather (Thomas) he must have sat just as he did in my drawing. A significant moment for me - memories coaxed out of him eventually started me off on our family trail.....

Drawing by Gloria Jarvis.

Oh, Grandpa Led Me A Dance!

It was a crisp December day, when, finding myself in Haddenham on the Bucks/Oxfordshire border, I looked across the village green my farming ancestors knew. That was their church, with the same pond and, a bit beyond, the great tithe barn where in Autumn they used to pay their tithes - and sometimes conveniently "forgot".

Christmas would be here in a week or two - just the time of year to contemplate their yuletide and I imagined them dragging the yule log across the threshold of their houses built with witchert, the name given to the Haddenham mud that set extremely hard and which, mingled with flint, produced very solid walls.

My mind went back to the Tudor forebears I had managed to unearth in Archives of the Record Office in Aylesbury - and I marvelled at the lucky breaks I had had to lead me to them, however many an impasse. The first setback was unwittingly caused by Grandpa:-

It was all through his getting just one fact wrong - but then, bless him, he had been asked to cast his mind back to the 1860s and his infancy, to remember what *his* grandfather, Thomas Jarvis, was like, from happy memories of holidays spent with him in Soulbury. Forty years later I referred to notes taken in my schoolgirl hand, and set off on the trail. Most of what he said was absolutely correct. So I believed him when he said "Grandpa (Thomas Jarvis) married Ann Durrant."

On the IGI there magically appeared a marriage, listed for two places, Stony Stratford and Leckhamstead - but wait a minute! 1783? Too early to be his grandparents. I leapt to the conclusion that he had confused the Jarvis generations, it must be his *great-grandparents*. Our Thomas, according to the census of 1851, was born in Luton in 1794. But in Luton registers he is shown as the son of William Jarvis, putting paid to my theory. Yet grandpa was so categoric in his statement. This Thomas (1) and Ann must be connected.

At the time, I thought that Thomas (1) must be uncle to my Thomas (2). Thomas (1) proved to have a younger brother, William, and that convinced me. It took some time to locate the origins of this couple, "wrongly" recorded in the IGI. Only, the banns were called in Leckhamstead, and they actually married in Passenham, Northants, just over the border from Stony Stratford.

Passenham registers revealed Thomas's (1) family. When his father, William, came to light, I thought I had found my 4 x great-grandfather. Thomas's and Ann's first born was christened William in 1784 and our ancestral William baptised his Thomas in Luton in 1794. It gave me a warm feeling that the "brothers" were obviously fond of each other.

In Passenham, father William was a carpenter, and according to the overseers' accounts, he made a living, by repairing houses, fashioning stairs, windows, bedsteads, ladders, rafters, floors, and coffins galore. He also seems to have been a sort of constable, paid 6d *for crying down the dogs in the churchyard* and 5s *for looking after John Bignell when he was in hott* for shooting a baliff. William was paid 3s for removing Hannah Teagle to Cosgrove and it also cost the overseers 10s for the couple and their horses at the tollgate.

William's wife, Frances, fostered a foundling, abandoned in a corner of the village called Wakefield Piece, hence the baby was called 'Little Wakefield'. Frances received payments for *a payre of britches and a pair of stockins for Little Wakefield, 2s 5d: fran: Jarvis for making little Wakefield a coat 1s: a payre of shoes for Lit Wakefield,* and so on.

In 1801, William and Frances were struck down with smallpox. They were moved to a house of isolation (two villagers were paid for taking them), where they were nursed in turn by their daughter and others, who were paid and supplied with victuals (meat, bread and beer). It took them from mid-April till November to recover. The doctor's bill for that year was £43-13s. William was never the same again, for he was paid a regular allowance. By 1804 it was 4s a week and in December he received 9s 6d to buy 6 ells of cloth. In 1810 he was getting only 1s weekly.

Sadly, I learned of his demise. On 2nd September 1810, his shroud was paid for 5s, the coffin cost 12s and 3s 6d was paid for beer and layers out and funeral. I shed tears for him.

Yet it proved that William Jarvis of Passenham was none of mine. It was long after that I discovered that my Thomas Jarvis (2) married Hannah Adkins, and it was her father, who married another Ann Durrant in Great Brickhill in 1787. But William Jarvis of Passenham must be someone's 4 x great-grandfather - and what a fascinating glimpse of village life these overseers' accounts have given me.

APPENDIX

A SHOT IN THE DARK - AND BACK TO DOOMSDAY

PACK MULES AND COUNTRY CART

A MEDIÆVAL CART. (OLD M.S.)

ROYAL CARRIAGE CONVEYING THE KING'S HOUSEHOLD: (OLD M.S.)

PILLION RIDING

CART OF THE TIME OF KING JOHN.

A SHOT IN THE DARK

Having a name of Norman origin can set off a train of wishful thinking all the way back to 1066. It is easy enough to top the family tree with Norman warriors, but tracing them is another matter, fraught with obstacles - due in part to one's inadequacies in Latin and Old English. The discovery of any pre-Tudor ancestors could be judged a bonus before the advent of parish registers.

Yet Haddenham's part of the world does, somewhere in the records, give a glimpse of a fifteenth century Richard Jarvis angry with a neighbouring farmer for diverting a stream away from his land. And although any link up with our direct kin is missing, the reappearance of the name Richard is worth noting as proof of an ongoing tradition from a remoter past. It hints of further Richards waiting in the wings.

Then one day, a certain Richard Gerveys of 1422 came to light, but in the village of Gayhurst, north-east of the county...and, from the previous century, a John Gervays of the neighbouring village of Stoke Goldington. They figure in a bundle of deeds of the Gayhurst Estate which was discovered in the cellars of Gayhurst mansion in the 1920s, and repaired and compiled by Dr. Fowler, Chairman of the Bedfordshire County Records Committee. He transcribed them from the original Latin and Old English, which makes for painless reading. They are in the Buckinghamshire County Record Office in Aylesbury.

From Richard's deed of a cottage we learn that he was a "tailour" living in church property--presumably making garments for religious houses. Imagine him travelling between many priories in the county. Imagine, too, his wife, Alice, busying herself at home, sewing away like a good helpmate. The deed states that the cottage was "in the gift of William Peke, chaplain". Perhaps he, also, profitted from the couple's workmanship--as may the bishop of Lavendon, who owned the tenement next door.

John Gervays, on the other hand, was a man of means. In 1365 he and his wife, Joan, came into a small estate at Stoke Goldington. His first deed of February that year states that John Wolf (a worthy of Horpole, over the border in Northamptonshire) "have confirmed to John Gervays and Joan his wife one toft and one acre of land and ten shillings rent in the village of Stoke Goldington which I had of the gift and feoffment of John de Morewell".

The second deed of October goes further: "Know all men by these presents that I John Wolf of Horpole have remised, released, and in every way for myself and my heirs for ever having quitclaimed to John Gervays and Joan his wife and their heirs or assigns all right and claim which I have, had, or may have in any way in the future in all the lands and tenements, rents and services and all other the appurtenancies which the aforesaid John Gervays and Joan hold in Stoke Goldyngton, Latheburi and Chicheley, which same lands and tenements rents and services were formerly of John de Morewell... "The chief witness was the Mayor of Northampton, and in the former deed among those who signed was John Nouwers of the Goldington family, lords of the place.

Now John de Morewell descended from the Goldington family; Peter de Goldington came over with the Conqueror. John's descent was through his mother, Lucy, the youngest daughter of Giles Revel, who married as her second husband, Robert de Morewell.

In the third deed held by John Gervays he grants to Joan, widow of John de Morewell, the use of a chamber with "false" chamber annexed, two gardens and a curtilage in Stoke Goldyngton to the same for life. This hints at a parentage between the widow and the beneficiaries of the estate-- perhaps Joan Gervays was the de Morwell daughter, and this her inheritance.

What I find intriguing is that the two deed holders, in Gayhurst and Stoke Goldington, are blessed with the Jarvis family names of Richard and John--and a surname the forerunner of Jarvis.

The fact that Gayhurst and Stoke Goldington are a long way from Haddenham does not present any difficulties for me. With each generation it would not have been possible for every son to find enough land to till in the same place--so they had to go further afield--and as the crow flies, Haddenham is not as far as you would think. They got around in those days!

There are no fifteenth century cottages left at Gayhurst at which to point and say: "So that's how it must have looked!"

Whereas much of the John Gervays estate at Stoke Goldington, up the road, can be visualised from the deed of 22nd February 1365/6, which sets out the dowager Joan de Morewell's living quarters--entitlement as dower--her "thirds", as it was termed.....one garden called le ympehey lying behind the said hall, together with one other garden lying behind the Grange, and one curtilage called le Morrine-orchard-- graphic in its brevity, poetic, too, a little cameo that also gives a clue as to locality in the phrase "lying behind the Grange", which in the Midddle Ages was the home farm. A vestige might be left...how to track it down...

Press cuttings from the Wolverton and North Bucks Express of August 8th 1969, in Aylesbury Reference library speak of an archaeological search for a Mediaeval convent in the area, and that, in the process, a farmyard was discovered, said to be of the Grange, once part of an ancient estate. Their finds included a farmyard well, pottery, roof tiles, spurs, horseshoes and ironwork. It is a moated site between Stoke Goldington and Hanslope, and known as Gorefields.

In the Victoria County History of Bucks mention is made of "A property in Stoke Goldington called in the late 16th century Gervays Place Manor derived its name from the family of John Gervays, who held land here in the late 14th century...The name perhaps survives in Jarvis Wood." Until more research brings its location to light, it remains an unsolved mystery.

I console myself with the visit I made to Stoke Goldington's Church of St Peters, where the 14th century couple would have worshipped. I stayed, a solitary, for most of an afternoon, basking in the haven of its churchyard, and jotting down my impressions as set out below.

Sharing the rise in the land with Church Farm is Stoke Goldington church--hid from the lane by a cluster of trees--till you seek out the gate and pass through, stepping into a Tudor haven--where Shakespeare's early summer flora of buttercups, lilac, hawthorn and laburnam gaze...stone walling, low, light and mellow enfolds this carpet-sward of green--its tombstones all at angles stand awry to send their ageless aura round the vibrant humming bees. Due south, a little wrought iron gate gives onto undulating fields of young and thrusting wheat, vanishing in perspective to the sky. I push the church door, enter in the footsteps of the past, and pass into the sanctum--its steady beating heart still welcoming a pilgrim who claims a filiation with two 14th century worshippers: John Gervays, Joan his wife. They came into a small estate but half a mile away--recalled in bosky fragments--still alive as Jarvis Wood.

Mummers, or enteitainers at Old English country revels.

A Norman noble wearing
tunic, over-tunic and
mantle.

Norman horsemen with lady riding pillion,

Villeins sowing and harrowing.

A Norman lady wearing
robe, mantle and head-veil.

THE HALL.

THE BOWER.

A FEELING IN ONE'S BONES AND
BACK TO DOMESDAY

Among the knights struggling with their horses to board the ships embarking for Hastings was William de Carun--who took his name from his native Cairon in Calvados.

It goes without saying that a knight bearing arms in Duke William's cause might expect a share of the spoils

KNIGHT.

when English land changed hands after the Conquest.
Especially if he chanced to have a friend at court as did William de Carun. Cairon was near Ryes, the family seat of the powerful Eudo the Dapifer who had been boyhood companion to William the Bastard, himself, and was now his most trusted advisor. It was then natural that William de Carun, living in the vicinity of Ryes, should be part of Eudo's knightly circle--and the great man, having the ear of the Conqueror, would use his influence to reward the loyalty of his knights. In fact, Domesday later shows William de Carun in possession of a generous acreage of land in Bedfordshire as Eudo's under-tenant.

The Bedforshire estate passed to William de Carun's eldest son, Roger, whose brother, Ralph, was vested by Henry I in the estate of Sherington in north-east Buckinghamshire. Ralph de Carun died some time before 1140, and the property

passed to his son, William, whose marriage to Ida, daughter of Hugh Bulli, produced two sons, at least...perhaps a third...and a daughter.

The eldest, Richard, with his future already mapped out as heir to the estate, was placed as page in the household of his father's great friend, Gervase Peynel of neighbouring Newport--the town later to be named after its lord as Newport Pagnel. I believe that William and Ida de Carun gave their second son the name of Gervase out of affection for their friend of Newport. Younger sons had to be found a role in life, too. And Gervase was barely in his teens when a living did present itself as parson of Sherington church.

It was a scheme thought up by his father. As squire of Sherington William had, in 1140, given its church to the monks of Tickford priory. It had proved an astute move for the future...he now asked that young Gervase be accepted as parson--and, despite his youth, they eventually agreed.

Although he took minor orders, Gervase does not appear to have celebrated mass very often, spending most of the time farming the church land. But he was always known as Gervase the Parson while there--from 1170 until 1227--a fair length of time. As yet, clergy were permitted to marry, but he observed the convention of priestly celibacy just the same. Being no saint, he found himself father to three bastards: Richard, John and Simon--John by a lady called Howizia, who was also free with other high born men in the locality.

Soon, with advent of surnames, Richard Son of Gervase became Richard Gervase--and John Son of Gervase, John Gervase.

And was Richard Gervase the forerunner of all those Richards descending in generations of Jarvis families all over Buckinghamshire? And how those names recur--Richard and John--as Jarvis, Gervis, Gerveys yeomen and husbandmen in parish registers all over the county--and over the border into Northamptonshire. They must be our distant cousins. Stemming from Gervase?

I should like to express my gratitude to Professor A.C. Chibnall for bringing Gervase to light in his extensively researched account of the Carun family of Sherington in his book: Sherington: Fiefs and Fields of a Buckinghamshire Village, which was published in 1964 by Cambridge University Press.

William of Sherington's letter confirming his gift of Sherington church to Tickford priory in 1140 (below). Thirty years later he endorsed this with a deed witnessed at court at Woodstock by the heir-apparent young King Henry, deputising for his father King Henry II who resided in France. At the same time the monks of Tickford granted to Gervase the living with its house and croft with buildings for life for

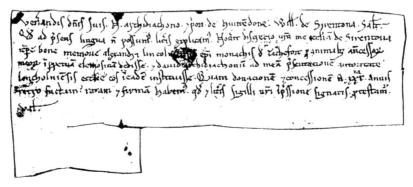

twenty shillings yearly rent--and so long as he lived dressed as a secular priest.

Before the Enclosure Award of 1797 at Sherington there still existed one of the great common fields which Gervase in his day called "the field towards the sun". I have the impression he was at one with the land and, with farming for around fifty five years, he must have had a constitution to match his Viking forebears' way back in time in Normandy.

Storing grain under the
direction of the bailiff.

Churning.

COMPAGNONS DE GUILLAUME À LA CONQUÊTE DE L'ANGLETERRE
EN MLXVI

Achard d'Ivri
Alevi
Altard de Vaux
Alain le Roux
Amaure de Dreux
Anquetil de Cherbourg
   de Grai
   de Ros
Anscoul de Picqvini
Ansfrei de Cormeilles
   de Vaubadon
Ansger de Montaigu
   de Senarpont
Ansgot
   de Ros
Arnould de Perci
   d'André
   de Hesdin
Aubert Greslet
Aubri de Couci
   de Ver
Auvrai le Breton
   d'Espagne
   Herteberge
   de Ianle
Azor
Beaudoin de Colombières
   le Flamand
   de Meules
Berenger Giffard
   de Toeni
Bernard d'Alençon
   de Neufmarche
   Pancevolt
   de Saint-Ouen
Bertran de Verdun
Beugelin de Dive
Bigot de Loges
Carbonnel
David d'Argenton
Drew de la Beuvrière
   de Montaigu
Durand Malet
Ecouland
Engenouf de l'Aigle
Engerrand du Rainbeaucourt
Ernais de Buron
Etienne de Fontenai
Eude Comte de Champagne
   Evêque de Bayeux
   Gui de Louf
   le Flamand
   de Fourneaus
   le Sénéchal
Eustache Comte de Boulogne
Foucher de Paris
Fouque de Lisorg
Gautier d'Appeville
Gautier le Bourguignon
   de Caen
   de Claville
   de Douai
   Giffard
   de Grancourt
   Hachet
   Heuse
   d'Incourt
   de Laci
   de Mucedent
   d'Omonville
   de Riebou
   de Saint-Valeri
   Tirel
   de Vernon
Geoffroi Albelin
   Bainard
   du Bec
   de Cambrai
   de la Guierche
   le Maréchal
   de Mandeville
   Martel
   Maurouard
   de Montbrai
   Comte du Perche
   de Pierrepont
   de Ros
   de Auneville
   Talbot
   de Tournai
   de Treill

Gerboud le Flamand
Gilbert le Blond
   de Blosseville
   de Bretteville
   de Budi
   de Colleville
   de Gand
   Malet
   Maminot
   Tibou
   de Venables
   de Wissant
Gonfroi de Cloches
   Mauduit
Goscelin de Cormeilles
   de Douai
   de la Rivière
Goubert d'Aufai
   de Beauvais
Guernon de Peis
Gui de Craon
   de Raimbeaucourt
   de Rainecourt
Guillaume Alis
   d'Angleville
   l'Archer
   d'Arques
   d'Audriu
   de l'Aune
   Basset
   Belet
Gilbert de Cibard
Guillaume de Beaufou
   Bertran
   de Biville
   le Blond
   Bonvalet
   de Bosc
   du Bosc-Roard
   de Bourneville
   de Brai
   de Briouse
   de Burigni
   de Canaigres
   de Cailli
   de Cairon
   Cardon
   de Carnet
   de Castillion
   de Ceauce
   la Cleve
   de Colleville
   Corbon
   de Paumers
   le Despensier
   de Ourville
   d'Ecouis
   Espec
   d'Eu
   Comte d'Evreux
   de Falaise
   de Fécamp
   Folet
   de la Forêt
   de Fougères
   Froissart
   Goulaffre
   de Letre
   de Louceiles
   Lovret
   Malet
   de Malleville
   de la Mare
   Maubenc
   Maudult
   de Molon
   de Monceaus
   de Moyers
   fils d'Olgeamc
   Pantou
   de Parthenai
   Peche
   de Perci
   Pevrel
   de Piquiri
   Poignant
   de Poillet
   le Poitevin
   de Pont-de-l'Arche
   Quesnai

Guillaume de Reviers
   de Sept-Meules
   Taillebois
   de Tocni
   de Yatteville
   de Youville
   de Ver
   du Vesli
   de Waremne
Guimond de Blangi
   de Tessel
Guinebaud de Balon
Guinemar le Flamand
Hamelin de Balon
Hamon le Sénéchal
Hardouin d'Escailles
Hascouf Musard
Henri de Beaumont
   de Ferrières
Herman de Dreux
Hervé le Berruier
   d'Espagne
   d'Helion
Honfroi d'Ansleville
   de Biville
   de Bohon
   de Carteret
   de Culat
   de l'Ile
   du Tilleul
   Vis-de-Louf
Huard de Vernon
Hubert de Mont-Canisi
   de Pont
Hugue   l'Ane
   d'Avranches
   de Beauchamp
   de Bernières
   du Bois-Hébert
   de Bolbec
   Bourdet
   de Brebeuf
   de Corbon
   de Dol
   le Flamand
   de Gournai
   de Grentemesnil
   de Guideville
   de Modene
   de Motat
   d'Ivri
   de Laci
   de Maci
   Maminot
   de Manneville
   de la Mare
   Mautravers
   de Mobec
   de Montfort
   de Montgommeri
   Musart
   de Port
   de Rennes
   de Saint-Quentin
   Silvestre
   de Vesli
   de Viville
Ilbert de Laci
   de Toeni
Ive Taillebois
   de Vesci
Josce le Flamand
Lanfranc
Mathieu de Mortagne
Mauger de Carteret
Maurin de Cade
Mile Crespin
Murdac
Néel d'Aubigni
   de Berville
   Fossard
   de Gournai
Normand d'Adreci
Osberne d'Arques
   du Breuil
   d'Eu
   Giffard
   Pestfereire
   du Quesnai

Osberne du Saussai
   de Marci
Osmond
Osmont de Vaubadon
Oure d'Addetot
   de Bercheres
Picot
Pierre de Valognes
Rabier d'Avre
Rainel d'Aunou
   Baignard
   de Bans
   de Bapaumes
   Basset
   de Beaufou
   de Bernai
   Blouet
   Botin
   de la Bruière
   de Chartres
   de Colombières
   de Conteville
   de Courianne
   de l'Estourni
   de Fougeres
   de Framen
   de Gael
   de Mauville
   l'Ile
   de Linquetet
   de Limesi
   de Marci
   de Mortemer
   de Moron
   d'Ouilli
   Paimel
   Pinel
   Pipin
   de la Pommeraie
   du Quesnai
   de Saint-Samson
   du Saussai
   Taillebois
   du Theil
   de Toent
   de Tourlaville
   de Tournerville
   Tranchant
   fils d'Unepac
   Vis-de-Louf
Ravenot
Renaud de Bailleul
   Croc
   de Pierrepont
   de Saint-Hélène
   de Torterel
Renier de Grimou
Renouf de Colombelles
   Flamard
   Pevrel
   de Saint-Valeri
   Vaubadon
Richard Basset
   de Beaumais
   de Bienfaite
   de Bondeville
   de Courcy
   d'Engagne
   L'Estourni
   Fresla
   de Meri
   de Neauville
   Poignant
   de Reviers
   de Sacqueville
   de Saint-Clair
   de Sourdeval
   Talbot
   de Yatteville
   de Vernon
Richard d'Andeli
Robert d'Armentières
   d'Auberville
   d'Aumale
   de Barbes
   Le Bastard
   de Beaumont
   le Blond
   Blouet
   Bourdet

Robert de Brix
   de Buci
   de Chandos
   Corbet
   de Courçon
   Cruel
   le Despensier
   Comte d'Eu
   Fromentin
   fils de Gerould
   de Glanville
   Guernon
   de Harcourt
   de Lorz
   Malet
   Comte de Meulan
   de Montbrai
   de Montfort
   Comte de Mortain
   des Moutiers
   Murdac
   d'Ouilli
   de Pierrepont
   de Pontcherdon
   de Rhuddlan
   de Romenel
   de Saint-Leger
   de Thaon
   de Toeni
   de Yatteville
   des Vaux
   de Veci
   de Vesli
   de Villon
Roger d'Aubernon
   Arundel
   d'Auberville
   de Beaumont
   Bigot
   Boissel
   de Bosc-Normand
   de Bosc-Roard
   de Breteuil
   de Buli
   de Carteret
   de Chandos
   Corbet
   de Courcelles
   d'Evreux
   d'Ivri
   de Laci
   de Lisieux
   de Meules
   de Montgommeri
   de Moyeus
   de Mussegros
   de Oistreham
   d'Orbec
   Picot
   de Pistres
   le Poitevin
   de Rames
   de Saint-Germain
   de Sommeri
Ruaud l'Adoube
Seri d'Auberville
Serlon de Burci
   de Ros
Sigan de Cloches
Simon de Senlis
Thierri Pointal
Thiel de Merion
Toustain
Turald
   de Grenteville
   de Papeilon
Turstin de Gueron
   Mantel
   de Saint-Hélène
   fils de Rou
   Tinel
Vauquelin de Rosai
Vital
Wedard

B'Aunrocher d'Angerville
de Bailloui
de Briquerville
Daniel
Savant
de Clinchamps
de Courcy
le Vicomte
le Tourneant
de Tilly
Danneville
D'Argouges
D'Auvay
de Briquerville
de Canneville
de Cugey
de Fribois
d'Horicy
d'Houdetat
de Methem
de Montflouet
d'Orglande
du Merle
de Saint-Germain
de Sainte-d'Aignaus
de Touchet
de Venois

● Guillaume de Cairon figuring in the list of knights in the Church of Our Lady at Dives-sur-Mer.

List of William's Companions

On August 17 1862, during an international academic meeting, the list was inaugurated. Excerpts:

"At half past twelve, many delegates from societies, towns and villages in Normanday and other provinces which gave fellow fighter to William in 1066, went in procession to the great market of Dives, task fully decorated for this ceremony and displaying a painting, in the style of the Bayeux Tapestry, showing William's fleet being built and the Norman army embarking before sailing to England.

Monsieur de Caumont, chairman of the French Society of Archaeology, declared the session open and delivered the main speech".

The names featuring on the list we give here are carved on the western wall of the nave of the church, inside, above the main entrance. The area they occupy is over 200sq feet.

This list was drawn up by the French Society of Archaeology, with the approval of Mgr. Didot, Bishop of Bayeux, Monsieur de Caumont being chairman of the Society, Monsieur Renier, Vicar of Dives, Count Foucher de Careil, member of the Conseil General, Monsieur Amet, Mayor of Dives.

"Two other lists have been carved: on the flagstones of Hastings Abbey and in the chapel of the chateau of Falaise (Calvados)."

MUGGETS and SYLLABUB

"You're for Parliament - I'm Royalist," the fine lady sailing by threw over her shoulder at me. Dressed in simulated brocade, her bare chest said it all - as, of course, did the rose in her hair. I knew that my long black velvet skirt and bodice with full sleeves slashed in 17th century style were befitting a lady of mature years whose family stood for Parliament - but that my frilled collar of broderie anglaise was decorative enough not to cast me as a puritan zealot.

Some of the gentlemen present were as tall as I'd ever seen - with enormous girth - made bulkier by the cut of their 1640 period costumes. A few are also members of the Sealed Knot, a society that enacts the battles of the Civil War. Fighting exercises physique and appetites, no doubt.

Invitation to this 17th century banquet was to commemorate the 10th anniversary of the John Hampden Society (created to revive recognition of the man, rightly named the Patriot - John Hampden). For according to many historians if he had not been fatally wounded early in the Civil War his flair for leadership would have outshone that of his cousin, Oliver Cromwell. But the skirmish with Prince Rupert on Chalgrove Field near Thame saw him leaving the fight slumped over his horse - till reaching Thame, his shot torn shoulder eventually proved mortal.

THE JOHN HAMPDEN SOCIETY
. . . honouring a great Englishman
10th Anniversary Banquet

27th October 2002 marks the 10th anniversary of the formation of the John Hampden Society. It is intended to mark this event by holding a 17th century banquet in the Great Hall of Hampden House, Great Hampden, where the inauguration took place a decade ago.

By happy chance 27th October this year falls on a Sunday, which is the only time Hampden House is available to us, so the banquet will follow the 17th century custom of dining early. It will commence at 1.30 pm and continue until 6.30 pm, with 24 courses (dishes) in 3 removes, as follows:

FIRST REMOVE	SECOND REMOVE	THIRD REMOVE
Gammon of bacon pie	Sausages cooked in claret	Cheddar
Leg of mutton stuffed with apricots	Roast pork	Brie
Kippers with onion	Lemon chicken	Fruit Tarts
Muggets	Venison pie	Minced Tarts
Pease Pottage	Grand Salad 2	Fruit Leathers
Grand Salad 1	Lob Lolly	Marmalade
Eggs in mustard sauce	Cucumber Salad	Fresh Fruit
Carrots with marigold flowers	Leafy Salad	Syllabub

Period musician Peter Bull wil play throughout the afternoon, and there may be other enterainments.

This banquet at Hampden House meant so much to me since 8 x Great Uncle Leonard had been yeoman in the Hampden household (hinted at in his Will of 1692) and hence would not fail to evoke a familial atmosphere; from the moment the mansion appeared through the distant beech trees, glowing in their Autumn colours, my senses quickened.

Rising among the woods, we were stopped in our tracks by a fallen tree across the road, and had to back down the lane and find another route. It was the Sunday of very high winds. When we got to the house itself there were more stricken branches - and whole beeches already chopped up ready to be carted away.

As I stepped over the ancient threshold I prepared myself for the menu of twenty four dishes - all from authentic 17th century recipes, and therefore an unknown quantity.

My first visit had been to an AGM of the society, when we had been given a conducted tour of the house by the owner, Tim Oliver - one feature being the brick parlour where John Hampden had been arrested for refusing to pay Ship Money.

A delicious 17th century punch whetted our appetites - until at 2 o'clock it was time to file into the banqueting hall, already alive with music. For our musician, Peter Bull, costumed and strung round with period instruments, drum, pipe and hurdy gurdy, was going through his repetoire of tunes and ballards of the Civil War.

The servants had lined up for our entrance, according to the custom. Their dress as domestics was so authentic that I couldn't help exclaiming: "How lovely!" and the woman I'd addressed it to bobbed a curtsey.

We found our places. Mine was next to a direct descendant of John Hampden (through the female line) Lord Hollenden. "I'm a bit out of breath," he said, "I've been chopping up the trees blown down in the gale!"

Let the banquet begin!.... the menu was to the order of First Remove, Second Remove, and Third, with dishes of such unusual names that one was avid to find out what a mugget was, for instance (and I never succeeded - only that it looked and tasted like a rissole, but round in shape). The syllabub was delicious.

The servants were still serving as the afternoon light began to fade. Candles miraculously appeared, for the power cut that had struck at midday was yet unrepaired. But candlelight lent a mellow period touch. It was time to retrieve my coat from the cloakroom.

And as I returned to the gathering I slowed down to take in the scene through into the banqueting hall, with the servants moving silhouettes against the candlelight. It was a moment to hold in the memory - a stepping back into the 17th century. Was long ago Uncle Leonard perhaps smiling from the shadows?

FROM THE WOMAN JOURNALIST
MAGAZINE OF THE SOCIETY OF WOMEN WRITERS AND JOURNALISTS

GLORIA JARVIS SMITH - A lady of Many Talents
by Margaret Crosland

Gloria Jarvis Smith is writing a family history which may provide the answer to an intriguing question. Just how large a part is played by heredity in the creation of a person who is not only a gifted artist, but also a poet, playwright, author and journalist?

Gloria's maternal forebears were Italian. Her grandfather came from Emilia - a craftsman who worked with the great Malatesta upon the mosaics in Westminster Cathedral. Her English father was a well-known graphics artist and illustrator. Spurred on by his example Gloria trained at St Martin's School of Art in London and later at the University of Florence. She graduated with honours and later became a lecturer on historic costume and an instructor in costume drawing at the Polytechnic in Regent Street.

As a teenager she also enjoyed writing, but it was when she married and moved to Brussels with her husband that the editor of the Brussels Times asked her for some pieces with a British flavour.

A successful painter by that time she had already won the Medaille d'Argent in Paris and the Italian Medaille d'Or. Much of her work was in permanent collections in Belgium in oils, water-colour, pastel, ink and gouache. Her portrait of Princess Paola of Liège had captured all the sweetness of her young subject, and a painting of Margaret Thatcher was said to be a favourite with that lady's husband.

Even so, the opportunity to work in another creative field was too good to miss. Gloria began to write short pieces for the Brussels Times and The Beacon (British Community News). She started with art and theatre reviews and reports on events of Belgo-British interest. Markets in Brussels and Walks in Brussels followed and tongue-in-cheek, A Look at Local Loos.

This was a suprising choice of subject for the resident painter at 'Old England' - a department store as exclusive as Fortnum and Mason, and an artist whose painting of a Frost Fair on the Thames had been exhibited at the Royal Academy and now hung beside a Rubens in the proud owner's private collection, but Gloria is a suprising person.

Quiet-voiced and modest she has a wicked sense of humour, sharp powers of observation, and a sparkling wit reserved for the most part for the enjoyment of her closest friends.

Encouraged by the success of her early writing she went on to produce short stories which were broadcast on BBC Radio 4 and the World Service. Her work also appeared in the annual exhibitions of manuscripts of l'Association Royale des Ecrivains Wallons. She then became a member of the Union Mondiale de la Presse Feminine.

On her return to England, Gloria settled in Canterbury. She was still painting, but a change of eyesight in middle age caused difficulties. She turned more and more to writing.

In 1990 she joined the SWWJ. Then she became Chairman of Canterbury Writers' Group, taking part in their annual performances of poetry and prose at the Canterbury Festival. One of her poems, Rose in the Martyrdom appeared in a Tributes in Verse anthology published in Poetry Now. For four years in succession her work was read at the London Drama Festival held at the Goodrich Theatre in Putney.

Gloria's interest in history has never flagged and a project dear to her heart is to act as a guide at Canterbury Cathedral, where she makes use of her fluent French and Italian when showing groups of foreign tourists round the historic site.

The BBC has accepted one of her plays for radio, but at present the family history is her major concern. In years to come this carefully researched work may prove invaluable to social historians. It traces the life of a family of English yeomen back to mediaeval times on her father's side. The exotic flavour of Italian blood adds mystery to the story.

Many of us would like to trace our ancestry, yet few of us have the patience to search through ancient documents, picking up snippets of information from Wills and parish registers. Gloria has done so, and the book, when finished, should provide a fascinating insight into the making of a writer.

Winter Edition 1999

The title section of "A Plan of the Manor of Soulbury" drawn up by Wm. Woodward in 1769 - and too charming to leave out. It was a few years before 4 x great-grandfather Richard Jarvis of Haddenham (1740-1810) settled in the parish at Hollingdon.

Courtesy of the Centre for Buckinghamhire Studies   (Photo Anne Jarvis)

97

The Story of this family in the 20th century is told in a separate publication:

A Jarvis Tapestry
Part II